D0908652

START SUPERVISING

E-70

START SUPERVISING

Third Edition

Howard F. Shout

The Bureau of National Affairs, Inc.
Washington, D.C. 20037

Copyright © 1972, 1977, 1984

The Bureau of National Affairs, Inc.
Washington, D.C. 20037

Second Printing August 1986
Third Printing December 1987

Cover art and book design by Cynthia Basil

Photography by John Ward

Library of Congress Cataloging in Publication Data

Shout, Howard F. (Howard Franklin), 1906–
Start supervising.

1. Supervision of employees. I. Title.
HF5549.S573 1984 658.3′02 84–12105
ISBN 0–87179–441–1

Authorization to photocopy items for internal or personal use, or the internal or personal use of specific clients, is granted by BNA Books for libraries and other users registered with the Copyright Clearance Center (CCC) Transactional Reporting Service, provided that $0.50 per page is paid directly to CCC, 21 Congress St., Salem, MA 01970. 0–87179–441–1/84/$0 + .50.

Printed in the United States of America
International Standard Book Number: 0–87179–441–1

658.302
S559

To My Wife—
a good supervisor

Contents

Foreword xi

1. **Sizing Up the Job 3**
   The Trial-and-Error Approach 3
   What Is Supervision? 3
   The New Supervisor 6

2. **Taking Charge 11**
   The Principle of Leadership 11
   Styles of Leadership 11
   Leadership Qualities 14

3. **Organizing the Work 19**
   Objectives 19
   Procedures 20
   Problems 21
   Changes 21
   Innovations 22
   Record Keeping 22
   The Computer: An Organizing Tool 25
   Organizing Is Basic 26

4. **Studying the People 29**
   The Need for Identity 29
   Individual Differences 30
   Evaluating the Work Force 30
   What Does This Mean for Supervisors? 33
   The Sum of the Parts 36

5. **Building the Team 41**

Team Spirit 41
Group Identity 41
Disaffection 42
Work Patterns 42
Automation 43
The Makeup of Groups 43
Transformation of the Group 45

6. Directing the Operation 51
Time-Use Patterns 51
The Startup 52
Work Assignments 54
Best Foot Forward 55
The Training Process 56
Coaching on the Job 58
Observation Trips 59
The Windup 62

7. Keeping the Lines Open 67
Up, Down, and Sideways 67
Rules for Good Communication 68
One-to-One Communications 69
The Call to Order 74
Public Speaking 75
Paper Work 75
Reports 76

8. Checking Results 81
Production Goals 81
Satisfactory Performance 82
Standards Setting 83
Employee Conduct and Performance 85
Work Procedures 88

9. Making Improvements 93
The Questioning Approach 93
Fact and Fancy 96
The Suggestion System 98

Inertia vs. Improvement 98
Union Participation 99

10. Dealing With Unions 103
Why Workers Join Unions 103
What Unions Can Contribute 104
The One in the Middle 104
How to Make Unionizing Unnecessary 107
Do's and Don'ts During the Organizing Period 107
The Management-Union Climate 109
A Test for Supervisors 110

11. Handling Problem Employees 115
Causes for Action 115
The Problem Drinker 116
Drug Use 117
Malingering 118
Troublemaking and Insubordination 119
Dress and Appearance 120
Personal Problems 121
The Young Worker 121
The Old Hand 122

12. Supporting the Organization 127
The Primary Responsibility 127
Staff Development 128
Working With Staff 129
Personal Development 130

13. Staying on Balance 137
Four Departments of Living 137
Handling Time Pressures 139

14. This Is Supervision 143

Foreword

Operations managers have been called by a good many names—some of them printable: supervisor, department head, crew chief, district leader, office manager, overseer, and others. No matter what the label, their primary responsibility has been the same—to see that the work gets out. This is one part of the job that hasn't changed over the years.

What has changed are the conditions under which managers operate. Today they work under more limitations than they did 50 years ago, and they deal with a freer work force. Tools and systems are now more complex, and the old styles of leadership are no longer getting results. The whole job has become more challenging and more difficult than it ever used to be.

To meet these changes managers are asking for all the help they can get, and some answers are beginning to come out. Scientists have had the work situation under a microscope and are reporting some useful findings. The problem is to move these ideas onto the job where they can be put into action. *Start Supervising* is an effort to bridge this gap.

The material was planned as a guide for new managers, but experienced people may also find it useful for review. The treatment has been kept short and direct to encourage readership and application. Acknowledgements are due all the sources from which ideas were drawn and especially to the many managers who have made contributions over the years. A special thanks must go to the good friends who gave the final product a needed pruning and paring.

Howard F. Shout
July 1984

1 · SIZING UP THE JOB

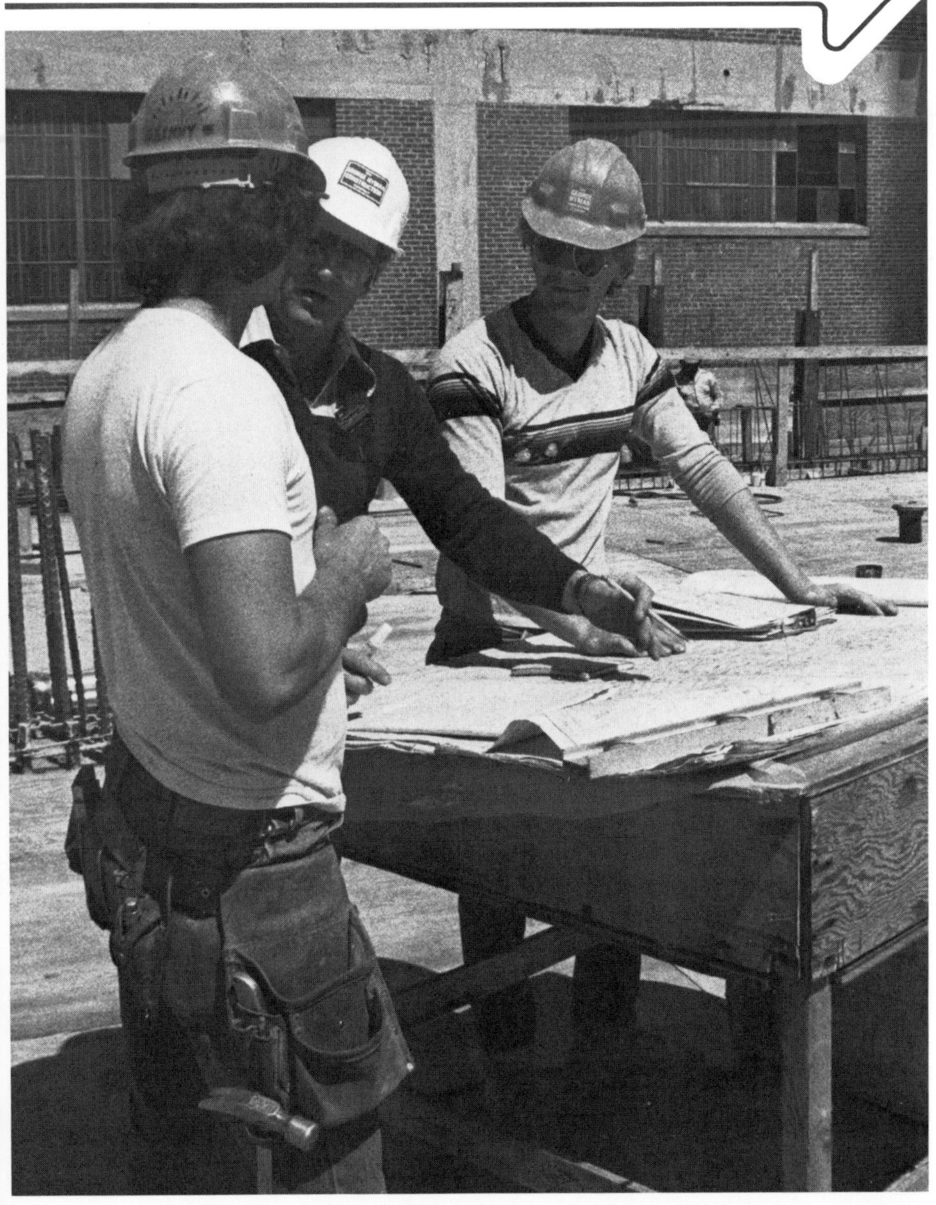

1 • Sizing Up the Job

When new supervisors take over their responsibilities, they move into a whole new territory. This is a good time for them to look over the situation before they get too far along. Without a little advance study, they can easily get into trouble. In the first place, there is quite a change from *doing* the job to *running* the job. Some are unable to make the jump and ask to move back. They are not ready to work by remote control through other people. As one manager put it, "The hardest lesson I had to learn was to keep my hands off the ropes." Supervision has to be recognized at the start as a new kind of work with new kinds of tools and materials.

THE TRIAL-AND-ERROR APPROACH

The situation is not helped by the training new supervisors usually get. When they ask what they are supposed to do, the answer in too many cases is, "You'll catch onto it in a few days. We know you can handle it or we wouldn't have put you in there." Not much help in getting a good start on the job!

New supervisors have usually been around the place for a while before they are promoted. Because they know the work, they are supposed to be able to step in and supervise it! In too many cases this does not prove to be enough. Effective front-line management is too important to be left to this kind of trial-and-error development.

WHAT IS SUPERVISION?

Supervisors' jobs come in all sizes. Some supervisors run the whole show, while others are work leaders who mainly carry out someone else's orders. Some do part of the work themselves and direct helpers on the side. There are no hard-and-fast rules about scope and responsibility. No matter where they start, though, good men or women can usually make their jobs expand by earning management's confidence. The top people have natural reservations until a new leader's ability and judgment are proven.

One thing holds true for supervisors anywhere—whether in the field, shop, or office, they are held responsible for other people's performance. When the work does not get out the door, they are the ones who have to answer. With this kind of accountability, supervisors need to know from the start what their jobs cover and how much authority they have to carry them out. The best way to get this straight is to sit down with the manager and talk it through. The list below can be a help in checking it out.

Responsibilities

There are a number of areas of responsibility a supervisor might be asked to cover. These may vary from one place to another, but in general the work falls under these headings:

Planning and Organizing
Laying out the work and deciding how to handle it.

Processing the Work
Assigning the work and supplying what's needed to get the job done.

Controlling the Operation
Keeping the work up to standard and checking on costs and materials.

Administering the Rules
Seeing that conduct and procedure are according to Hoyle.

Keeping People Informed
Communicating with and listening to staff—up and down the line.

Making Improvements
Finding better ways for doing the work—solving job problems.

Handling Personnel Matters
Administering time off, benefits, pay, change of jobs, overtime, and other personnel functions.

Training and Development
Breaking in new people, upgrading, building morale, planning replacements.

Monitoring Safety and Security
Preventing trouble. Dealing with accidents or illness. Safeguarding equipment and supplies.

Serving as Representative
Acting for the group or the organization as required.

Review these functions with your manager and find out what is expected. Some managers like to have everything cleared with them at the start. And some like to keep it that way. In any case, managers need to be kept informed about problems and developments. Their own plans may be affected, and they may need to notify others in the organization.

Authority

One point to be settled is the amount of authority the supervisor will be handed to carry out responsibilities. This should be stated for each of the 10 areas listed. Does the supervisor order the supplies, or does somebody else sign the requisitions? If he or she has the authority, what's the dollar limit? How about firing people, raising pay, giving time off, holding meetings, changing procedures? All these questions and others need to be answered in clear terms.

In general, there are two levels of authority: the authority to go ahead and take action and the authority to recommend what ought to be done. In either case, the supervisor is expected to keep higher levels informed about what happens after an action is taken. Results need to be reported and records kept on any matters of importance. Some supervisors keep a log book, the same as on shipboard. This allows for ready review whenever needed—and sometimes it is needed frequently.

THE NEW SUPERVISOR

New supervisors are usually on the spot during their first few weeks on the job. Mainly, people want to see how they will manage themselves under pressure. As the old phrase goes, "Will they *grow* with responsibility or just *swell*?"

Unless there are special problems, this is not a time to make changes or start throwing weight around. Supervisors are in a role that is different from being part of the group, and they have to establish a whole new set of relationships. There may be problems trailing along from the way things used to be. Former cronies may expect special treatment and be resentful if they do not get it. Experienced people will be jealous if they were by-passed. A certain amount of kidding is to be expected along with exaggerated deference. Remarks will be heard like, "Look out, here comes the brass," or "How does it feel to be a big shot?" Easy, steady good nature is the best way to meet the situation. As a matter of fact, steadiness is the main key to success in handling a group.

The Job Situation

This is the time to study the whole work structure from a supervisor's point of view. You may have been a member of the group before, but this was like riding along while somebody else drove the car. Now you are in the driver's seat and will have to deal with the traffic, watch the signs, check the map, and get everybody safely through to the end of the trip.

First, the supervisor should know what all the jobs require. This does not mean becoming a star on every operation, but you will need to know enough to train new people, correct mistakes, and recognize good performance. The manager of a ball team is not expected to play all positions, but is supposed to know how they should be played.

Second, the supervisor should be familiar with the tools and equipment required to do the job. A reasonable mastery of all of them is part of the necessary know-how. A good record in handling one of the jobs gives the group confidence that the supervisor knows the problems and can talk shop. This is important at the first and second levels of management, where supervisors deal directly with operations. Jobs and equipment, however, are only part of the story.

Third, the supervisor will need to study the layout and facilities, observe methods, check on operating standards and safety conditions, see how supplies are ordered and stored, and look for the possible problem spots in the whole procedure.

And, fourth, the new supervisor should give attention to his or her backup resources. What staff and service people are available? How is medical help called when needed? How about equipment breakdowns? And so on down the line. What manuals and guidebooks are around for reference, and what do they cover? What files are kept, and what is in them?

The Organizational Structure

There is still more to uncover, and previous experience around the place will not serve the purpose.

How do the supervisor and the work group fit into the organization? How does the supervisor deal with staff people from the front office and others in the line up? Who calls the shots, and what is the best way to proceed in order to get the work out as and when needed? If there is a union, how is its cooperation obtained and what are the limits? And one important item: Where does the supervisor check for a decision if the boss is not around?

The Work Group

The people that form the work group are the real materials to be worked with, and everything about them will be important. What can be learned about the people in the group? The personnel files and records will give some of the background. What are their abilities and experience? What are their outside activities? Length of service? Age? Potential? Work history? Attendance? Health? What kind of group are they, and how do they stack up with other groups in the place? How did the previous supervisor handle them, and is a different approach needed?

Preparation Time

All of this information cannot be picked up in a day or even several days. While sizing up the situation, the new supervisor will want to keep the work going along pretty much as it was. The aim of this lead time is to allow the new supervisor and management to come to a clear understanding on all aspects of the new position. This is the job and the results wanted; this is what the supervisor has to work with; and this is the way the supervisor can plan to take hold.

With full knowledge of the new duties and the direction to head in, you are set to take over in full. Preparation has been completed, and the real job of managing can begin.

Check List... sizing up the job

1. List your responsibilities.
2. Get agreement on your authority for each item.
3. Check work standards to be met.
4. Learn jobs and equipment.
5. Study layout and procedures.
6. Determine work practices of your manager.
7. Size up the rest of the organization.
8. Analyze the group and its members.
9. Determine what records are kept and what reports are required.
10. Consider changes—but go slow on initiating them.

2 · TAKING CHARGE

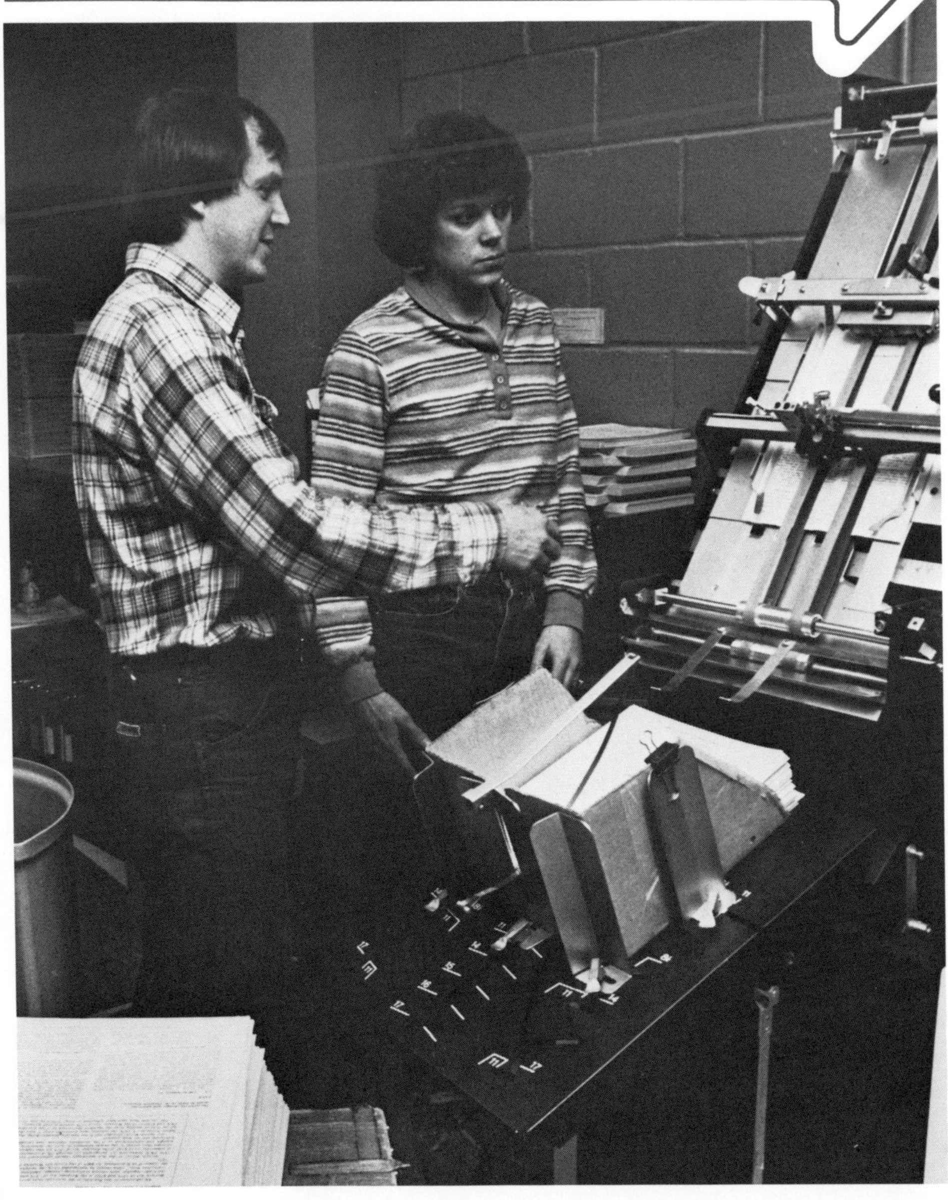

2 • Taking Charge

Taking charge means establishing leadership, and this needs a little time. Supervisors do not ride in on white horses and order the troops to parade. Most of them take over their positions quietly and without much show. Nobody respects the boss who acts like a big shot—at least, not until it is deserved. The best approach at the start is steady attention to business and a confident manner. In fact, this is a good pattern to follow all the way through.

THE PRINCIPLE OF LEADERSHIP

What are the specifications for a good leader? The most important one is that, after the leader is placed in charge, things begin to come out right. Workers want to be part of a successful operation. Whatever feelings a football team may have about the quarterback, they will back him if he can move the ball. A group wants to serve under a boss who can get the work out and is listened to by the front office.

Assuming the role of leader comes in two stages. First, management hands the supervisor a set of responsibilities and the authority to go with it; but management cannot confer the badge of leadership. This has to be earned from the workers themselves. Getting their support is the second stage. One field foreman put it this way: "When I say, 'Let's go,' and head for the truck and nobody follows me, that's when I find out I'm not leading."

STYLES OF LEADERSHIP

We hear much talk today about bosses who drive instead of leading their groups. This does not state all the facts a supervisor needs to know in order to develop his or her own style. Different elements in the picture call for different styles of leadership. A supervisor needs to get the feel of these variables before deciding which is the best pattern to follow. No one would question that a group of raw young workers requires a different approach from a team of skilled hands. A staff of scientists in a laboratory is not likely to respond to the same handling that a construction gang or a roomful of office workers might accept. The kind of group, the type of work, and the makeup of the supervisor will all have some effect on deciding the style of leadership. One fact we do know: the wise leader uses authority sparingly, especially today.

Contemporary Roles

Supervisors now have less absolute authority than they once possessed. It has been tempered by laws, unions, and social pressure. Management has stepped in, too, and placed limitations on supervisory roles for the protection of its employees. What we have now is a free labor force which is able to move around from job to job and which has a higher educational background than it did in the past. The immigrant workers of an earlier day are gone, and a home-grown corps of producers has taken their place. Some values may have been lost in this transition, but new ones have more than made up the difference. Workers today can deal with more complex equipment and procedures than their predecessors could. Productivity is higher, and we have moved into the computer age without too much trouble.

Handled right, there is no more effective production unit in the world than a modern work group with full equipment and the know-how to use it. Handled wrong, the same group can create more problems than anybody can handle. Every supervisor knows that a work group with problems could break the job if it wanted to and the trouble could not be pinned on any one cause. There would be lost parts and delays and rework until somebody upstairs asked for answers.

The Essentials

The old Bull o' the Woods used to think fear was the best approach. Keep 'em running scared so they don't have time to think. Outsmart 'em and outyell 'em. This worked in the old days but is not so effective in these times.

Others take the easy way out. They make like wet noodles. One supervisor said her job was just to keep "the girls" happy. "Let's Give the Company Away" is a popular song, especially with supervisors who get moved back to the ranks whenever work gets slack. Soft supervision does not work today, except possibly for a short period.

The supervisory approach with the best chance is based on respect—not fear or easy handling. And respect works both ways. Supervisors earn respect by the way they handle themselves and their part of the job. In turn, they give respect to the people under them for the part they play. One way to show respect for the group is by letting them in on things.

The leader who uses fear as a primary tool gets blind obedience, but never cooperation. Intelligent cooperation comes when workers are kept informed and have a chance to put in some of their own ideas.

Patterns of Decision Making

There is a range of workable leadership patterns which will earn the cooperation of workers with varying degrees of success.

Pattern No. 1, Supervisor Decides

The supervisor works out the plan, then tells the group what to do, how to do it, and why the decision was made that way. The supervisor answers questions and starts action.

Pattern No. 2, Supervisor Consults

The supervisor outlines the situation for the group and asks for their ideas. The supervisor considers their suggestions, decides upon the best plan of action, and then informs the group accordingly.

Pattern No. 3, Supervisor Shares

The supervisor outlines the situation for the group. The supervisor and group members exchange their ideas and then decide together what course of action to take. Here, the supervisor shares the decision-making responsibility.

Most good supervisors use all three of these approaches depending on the situation and the kind of group involved. Pattern No. 1 takes the shortest time, but Pattern No. 3 gets the best all-round support from the workers. The more say they have, the more they try to make the results come out right.

Whichever method is used, it is still the supervisor that carries the responsibility for whatever is decided. For this reason, Pattern No. 2 is favored by a good many leaders as a way to keep control and still give the group a part in the action.

The Patterns at Work

For example, a special job comes in. It has to be done right away, but the regular work still needs to get out. The supervisor can figure the best way to handle the problem and tell the group (Pattern No. 1); or call the troops together, lay out the facts, get their ideas, and then decide what to do (Pattern No. 2); or talk it through with them so they can all work out the answers together (Pattern No. 3). Even if the group is scattered the same system can be used, working with one or two people at a time. The more support wanted, the more necessary it is to move away from No. 1. And on any problem involving change, where people may begin to feel pushed around, the supervisor will be well advised to move to Pattern 2 or Pattern 3.

LEADERSHIP QUALITIES

We have talked about leadership methods, but what about the makeup of leaders? Don't some people have natural qualities that make other people want to follow along? Before we try to answer this, a few preliminary points need to be covered.

There is no one recipe for producing good leaders. They come in all types—plain, fancy, and assorted. A good fit for one position may be a failure in another. The one who can take over on a camping trip may be no good for running a sales campaign or a computer system. A self-starter who can get a business going may not be the best one to keep it operating after it is established. And a woman may have the right touch for some situations where a man would have problems.

There is no need to put yourself down, as they say, because you do not have a commanding personality or a booming voice. Flashy individuals may look good at the start, but the main question is how they will set with their people over the long pull. The leader who lasts is the one the group finds it can live with day in and day out.

What are the qualities that give an individual a good start toward leadership? One essential would have to be good *judgment*, the ability to cope successfully with situations that come up normally on the job. After all, there is no substitute for sound working intelligence.

A second quality would be a kind of concern for the people in the group. The experts call this *consideration*, and it is a quality any leader can develop. The trick is for the supervisor to think and act more like an assistant to help the workers get the job done, smooth the way, see that they have what they need, make suggestions, and give support. And, this works whether supervising a farm or a factory operation, a gang of gandy dancers on the railroad, or a corps of lab technicians.

A third quality that marks the leader is an ability to get things organized. Again, the experts have a word for this; they call it *structure*. This is a kind of built-in capacity for planning ahead and laying out the steps for reaching the objective. People will follow a leader who runs a program that is well planned and well administered. The next section will show how important this is for success in supervision.

Check List... taking charge

1. Move into the job with confidence.

2. Earn respect—do not try to force it.

3. Fit leadership patterns to the group.

4. Keep the group informed.

5. Talk over job problems.

6. Get facts before deciding action.

7. Admit mistakes.

8. Be natural and consistent.

9. Show consideration.

10. Support your group.

3 · ORGANIZING THE WORK

3• Organizing the Work

Most supervisors inherit a going operation when they take over their jobs. The procedures are all established, the workers know their business, and the equipment is in running order. As long as no changes are made, organizing duties are limited to lining up the jobs for the day or week and posting the schedules. This is pretty much a routine process, but some supervisors still seem to make it come out better than others.

When George Washington was operating his Virginia farms in 1789, he remarked in a letter to John Fairfax about this difference between overseers:

> Take two managers and give to each the same number of laborers, and let these laborers be equal in all respects. Let both these managers rise equally early, go equally late to rest, be equally active, sober and industrious, and yet, in the course of the year, one of them, without pushing the hands under him more than the other, shall have performed infinitely more work. To what is this owing . . .?

The answer Washington was looking for was probably fairly simple. One manager was a better planner and organizer than the other. He moved his crew steadily from one job to another. After all, most good organizing is plain common sense; it just has to be applied. Here are a few ideas to point the way.

OBJECTIVES

Planning is the start of any organized approach to a job. This is the *think* stage before the supervisor gets into any action at all. Answers are needed for a series of questions:

What has to get done? (Handle so many customers—Produce so many units—Type so many letters, etc.)

What standards have to be met? (Quality—Time schedule—Cost limits)

What do we have to work with? (People—Equipment—Supplies)

What is the best way to do the job? (Work methods—Material handling—Output checks)

How will we split up the work? (Who does what jobs? Who will be in charge? What outside help is needed?)

Most of the time when a job goes wrong, not enough thinking about objectives was done beforehand. Every operation needs planning even when it looks routine. Conditions can change from one project to another.

The overall objective is the highest output in the shortest time at the lowest cost. And this means holding slack time down without making people feel pushed. The work should move along smoothly. For example, one woman, head of a tree-trimming crew, always started with a layout of the day's work for her crew. When the first job was under way, she left a leadman in charge and moved ahead to line up work at the next location. She checked with property owners, sized up the projects, and had the job waiting when the crew moved in.

PROCEDURES

Nothing keeps the work going like the team that knows its business. This means that everybody has been trained and procedures have been set for the group to follow: "This is the way the job is done." "Here is what you do in case you have trouble." The more supervisors have to be on top of the job, the less preparation they have given their people. Well-written operating manuals and other guides can take care of nine-tenths of the daily work.

With procedures established, the supervisor's job is to stay out of the way and keep available for the special problems—in other words, to manage by exceptions. The rest takes care of itself. The basketball coach sees that the team has thorough training and plenty of practice.

They are well grounded in the fundamentals and drilled on the plays. After that they go through the game automatically unless some special situation comes up on the court. That's where the coach comes in—on the exceptions.

PROBLEMS

Problems are part of every supervisor's job, and they come from two directions—inside and outside the work situation itself. Inside problems are the normal headaches. Workers are absent, equipment breaks down, supplies run short, mistakes are made, and so on. Other problems come at the supervisor from outside. Specifications get changed, a heavy load of orders comes in, a rush job has to be put through, or supplies are not delivered on time. Some kinds of work have their own peculiar difficulties. A field operation may run into bad weather, or a traffic jam may hold up a transportation schedule.

The point is that these are problems the supervisor can expect, and so be ready to make the right move at the right time. A restaurant manager has food in reserve when an unexpected crowd of customers comes in. The foreman on a farm operation has inside chores lined up for the hands when the weather stops outside work. An able supervisor in any line of work is prepared for the normal upsets that come in any business.

CHANGES

New developments today come thick and fast, and supervisors are called on frequently to reorganize their work. A change may be as simple as putting in a new piece of equipment, but it can also be a major one that requires complete revision of layout and procedures.

Reorganizing goes on every day in a progressive business. A storm door manufacturer decides to introduce a new custom line. A food chain moves its meat operation from personal orders to self-service. An accounting office shifts from regular posting procedures to a computerized system. All of these call for the supervisor to restudy the flow of work, design a new set of jobs, retrain, and establish a different system of checks and controls.

INNOVATIONS

Sometimes as a supervisor, you will be assigned to lay out a whole new procedure from A to Z. This is a real challenge to your organizing ability and your creativity. You may be asked to set up a production line or establish a branch at a different location. To plan your approach, some familiarity with work production will be important.

For one thing, you will need to identify your "unit of work." This is the single item that an operation was set up to process. It may be a finished part in a machine shop, a shipping order in a warehouse, a tray-service in a hospital, a letter in a business office, a shirt in a laundry, or a sale in a showroom.

You should also study the work flow in your operation. Every service or production process has a start and each has a finish. Different operations are performed until output of the unit is completed. Flow charts can be filled in to show this movement. The objective is to lay out the operation so the movement of work can be rapid and steady.

Scheduling should be geared to the shortest possible time for processing a unit. Limiting factors are the number of units demanded, the time allowed, the methods used, and the men, materials, and machines available. Gantt charts have proved effective in shop production, and program evaluation and review technique (PERT) charts, a refinement of the critical path method, have proved useful in construction and other large-scale projects where many people and many dollars are involved. Figures 1 and 2 are simplified versions of the Gantt and PERT methods of scheduling the construction of a storage shed in a public park.

RECORD KEEPING

A way of checking on work progress is also needed. Every run or order requires a full report. In job shops a tag moves with the unit to register work done and time involved. Hospitals, service garages, travel agencies, and all other businesses require records of work provided. These are necessary controls to keep the business operating successfully. There are other factors to be considered, but these are the main elements.

What we are after in work organization is the optimum combination of people, machines, and materials, so that we get the best possible

Figure 1. **Simplified Gantt Chart**

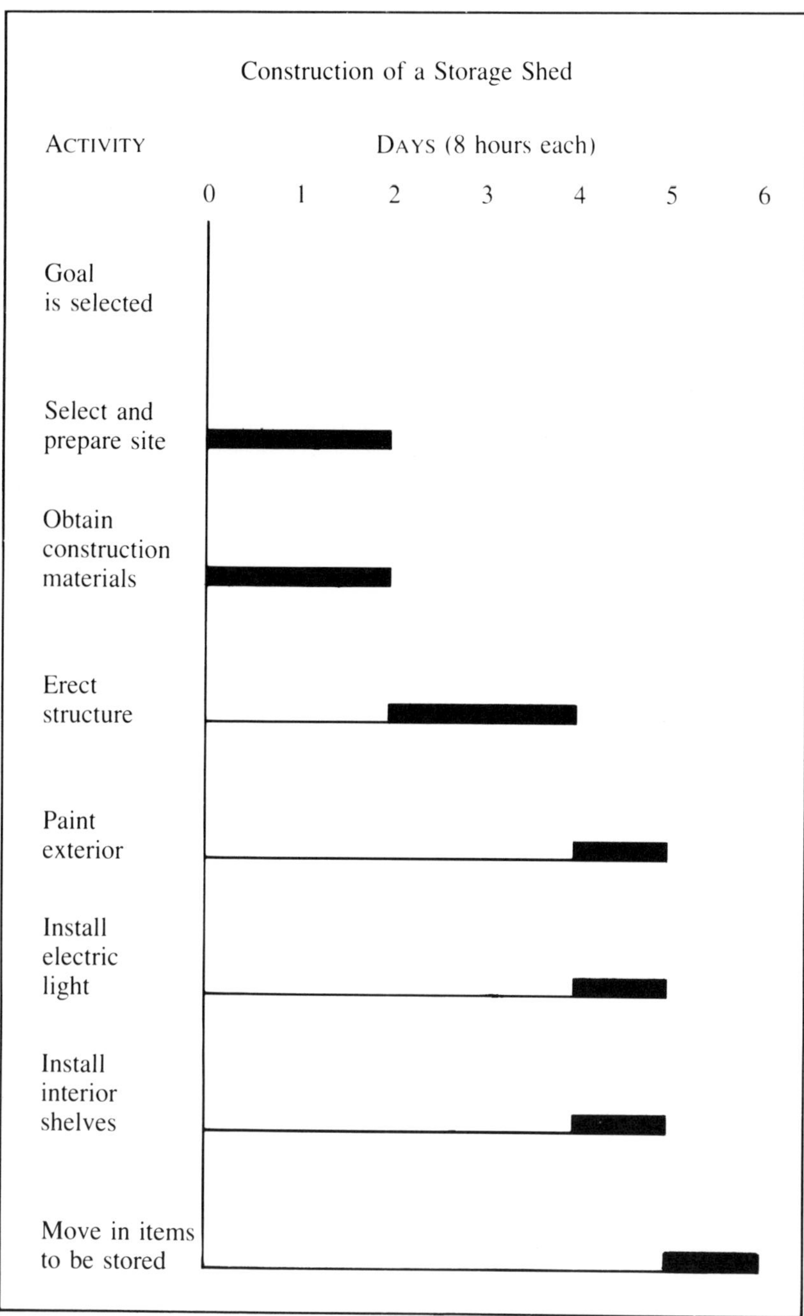

Figure 2. **Simplified PERT Chart**

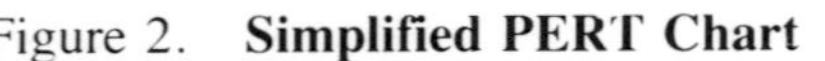

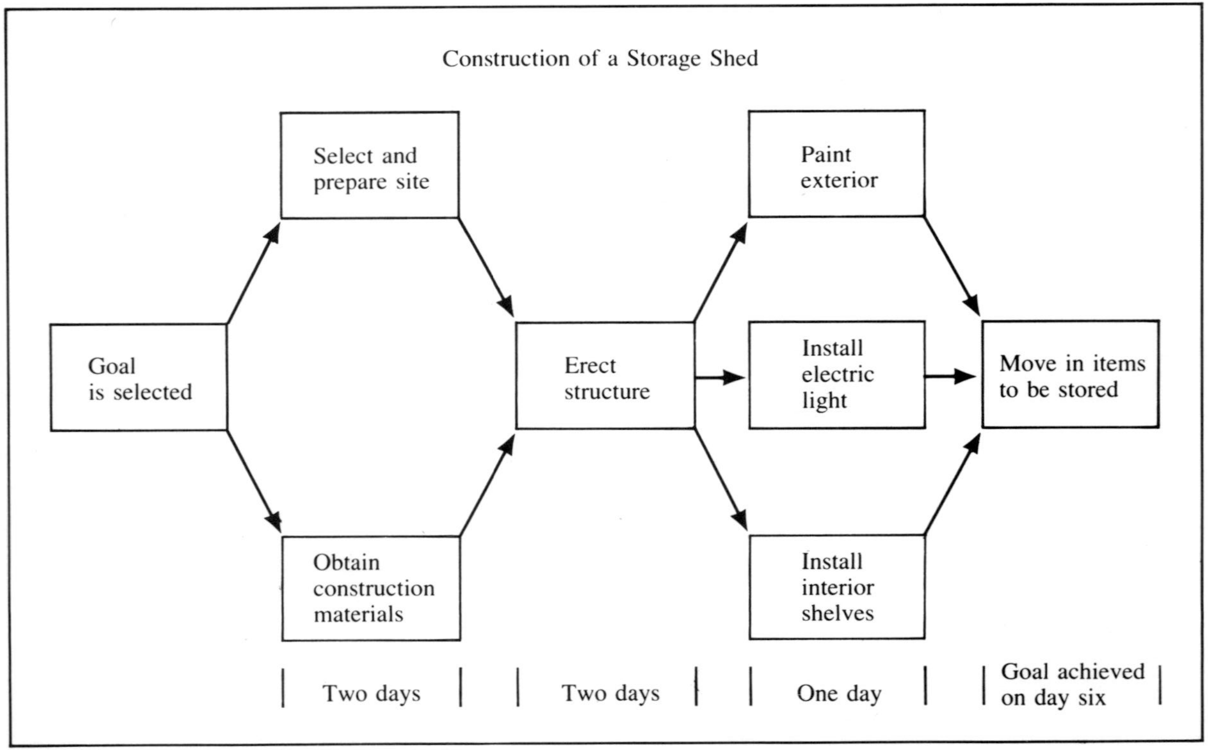

output for the least money in the fewest minutes. In a restaurant operation, for example, the manager works out kitchen procedures and food service that will place an appetizing meal before the customer and clear the table as quickly as possible for the next one coming in the door.

THE COMPUTER: AN ORGANIZING TOOL

Supervisors circle around this newcomer like strange dogs on first contact. They are not sure whether it is friend or foe. Actually, electronic data processing can do much to make the work easier and save headaches. It can help in planning and controlling almost any operation. Application, of course, is best when it covers a complete flow of work. The supervisor who handles only one phase of an operation can seldom justify a study, but may be able to influence higher level managers and other supervisors to move in this direction.

If the whole operation can be involved and a computer is available for use, the best approach is in three stages. First, get an introduction to computer language and forms. Find out how the system feeds back information. The shortest way is to take a course. Second, spend some time with a computer expert to analyze the operation. If it can be arranged, bring the expert to the work location. Decide what kind of information would be useful and how to supply raw data for the computer to process. And third, when the reports start coming back, spend another session with the expert to analyze them. Make any changes that are necessary to draw out the needed information, and let the feedback pour in.

What supervisors can get from computers are fast, hard facts about every measurable part of their work: costs per unit, performance per man or machine, records on quality, comparisons by time periods, pinpoints on trouble spots and bottlenecks. The big plus is in better data for planning and faster checking of the whole operation. In the past, supervisors based their decisions on *feel*; with computers they can base them on *fact*. The manager who gets a supervisor's proposals for new equipment or a change in setup is more apt to listen when the facts are there to support the recommendations.

ORGANIZING IS BASIC

Behind every going operation is an organizer—somebody to work out the procedures and pull resources together to get the project rolling. Organizing is the first step in managing, and this applies to homes, farms, clubs, companies, and all other enterprises. The process may look easy, but there always seems to be a shortage of people with the skills needed. It is estimated that about 10,000 businesses fail every year—mostly for lack of sound organizing.

Supervisors have other roles to play that are as important as organizing. One of these is dealt with in our next section: knowing the workers and developing their potential.

Check List... organizing the work

1. Plan ahead!
2. Set work objectives, decide on methods, set up, test run, and check results.
3. Work toward highest output in shortest time at lowest cost with least pressure.
4. Lay out procedures to be followed—then deal with exceptions.
5. Keep system under study—analyze work flow.
6. Use computer, where available, to get facts and improve system.
7. Keep full records.
8. Stand ready to meet expected problems.
9. Be prepared to reorganize for major changeovers.
10. Build sound organizing habits.

4 · STUDYING THE PEOPLE

4 • Studying the People

Supervisors with costly equipment in their charge will analyze it to find its capacity and operating characteristics. Most of the time, though, they fail to give the same attention to the people they supervise. Each worker represents a sizable investment over a 40-year work span—from a quarter-million to a million dollars. Failure to analyze workers is bad practice and can be costly to the operation.

"Know your people" is a familiar phrase, and most supervisors recognize its importance. The trouble is they go only part way in carrying it out. They learn names and size up employees' skills on the job, but they leave to chance and casual contacts the filling in of the rest of the picture.

THE NEED FOR IDENTITY

Lack of time and fast turnover are handicaps in getting to know members of a work group. Human beings in a mass lose their identity, and supervisors soon begin to think of them as all pretty much alike. When one leaves, they call up and say, "I just lost a worker. Send me another one." What they come to feel is that one peg can be pulled out and another shoved in without regard for shapes or sizes.

As one supervisor put it, "They're coming in and going out all the time. The back of one is the face of another." And it is true that turnover can wear down even a conscientious manager. Also true, however, is the fact that time spent working with newcomers can go a long way toward keeping them on the job. All they need is a feeling of being treated as individuals. A first step in this direction is for supervisors to size up each man or woman separately.

INDIVIDUAL DIFFERENCES

No two people are alike, and this is, of course, what makes them individuals. They are as different as fingerprints. Each man or woman has a unique and personal collection of abilities, list of wants in life, and package of feelings to carry around. All of these can affect their work and the way they fit in with the group. Supervisors know this, but their people's behavior still puzzles them. What they would like are some ways to hold individuals up to the light for examination.

EVALUATING THE WORK FORCE

There are questions that run through all managers' minds as they look at their employees. Why does one cooperate and another one fight authority? Why do some put out a day's work and others avoid it? Why is this one a chronic absentee and that one a griper? Why does the new woman have trouble following instructions? Is this man lazy, or is the job wrong for him? Why does the work come so easy for some and hard for others? How can a little ambition be built into the good ones? The list would be endless if we tried to cover all aspects of the behavior of people on the job. And behind the other questions, supervisors have one they do not express openly: Why can't more people be like me?

Let's look for some answers.

Individual Capabilities

Each person brings to the job a different set of skills and abilities, and the supervisor has the task of fitting them all into the work situation. The employees who come into a supervisor's group did not all have the same start and development in life. People are born equal only in their rights as human beings. In everything else—looks, build, intelligence, special talents, and a host of other characteristics—they are all products of their ancestry and conditions of growth. What they acquire in blood, brains, and brawn is what they have to build on for the rest of their lives.

One thing supervisors should understand from this is that they can always expect some workers to be less capable than others—not because they are trying to be slow or inept but because that is all they have to offer on that particular job. There may be other jobs where their abilities would fit better.

Performance Standards

Almost everyone can be taught simple skills, and practice will bring some improvement, but differences can be expected even after long experience. Normal activities like driving a car or hammering a nail will vary with muscular coordination, eyesight, depth perception, and other factors. Some companies use tests to find whether applicants can fill their jobs. For the ones that make it, the supervisor provides training. Job experience is expected to do the rest to bring them up to standard.

Minimum performance standards on most jobs are geared to the low-average worker. Supervisors can expect many of their people to do average work simply because more average people will be recruited for the job. Abraham Lincoln remarked that the Lord must have loved ordinary folks because He made so many of them.

If the supervisor gets a few high producers, he can consider it a bonus because outstanding workers usually tend to slow down and stay with the group. They are afraid of looking like eager beavers and becoming unpopular as a result. Slow ones, on the other hand, may do their best and still not be able to reach the average. If they fail to meet minimum standards, of course, they should be moved off the job. Otherwise, standards become meaningless.

Motivation

So, there are differences in makeup and ability that start right from birth. But there are other ways people can differ, and one of these is of primary importance to supervisors, namely, the difference in what moves people to act, to work, to do anything. Psychologists call this motivation. Supervisors put it in terms they are concerned about: What will get employees to pull their weight on the job?

The Money Factor

Human beings are not like typewriters; they do not have standard keyboards. Press the same key for two individuals, and you may get different responses. Probably nothing in the supervisor's job is more bothersome than the unpredictability of people.

Part of the trouble may be that the supervisor is putting too much reliance on pay as the great mover of people. One analyst has pointed out that an employer can buy a person's time, attendance, and work but the employer cannot buy loyalty, support, and enthusiasm. These added commitments have to be earned.

And that's the problem—how do we earn them? Here are some questions that might point to an answer:

Why do supervisors themselves usually show qualities of enthusiasm, loyalty, and initiative? Is it the pay they receive or some other satisfaction they get from being a supervisor, such as problems to face and responsibilities to meet?

If all employees had the same pay as supervisors, would they show the same qualities? Or if their pay were doubled, would they work twice as hard?

Why do some people leave well-paying jobs to go back to farming or start small businesses—even for less income? Why do some stay on jobs where they feel needed and turn down better offers?

What does everybody want from life, anyway?

Needs Satisfaction

Most people have three needs in common and spend their lives trying to satisfy them. Supervisors who do what they can to build these satisfactions into the job will go far toward producing an effective work team. The three needs are for physical, social, and personal satisfactions.

Physical needs are first in the basic list, and these are easy to understand. All workers want enough food, clothing, and shelter for themselves and their dependents, and assurance that these will continue to be available in the future. Individuals will do what they have to do to satisfy their physical requirements. When these basic needs are taken care of, they are ready to reach for social satisfactions.

Social needs run a close second in importance for people. They want the approval, acceptance, and affection of friends, families, and fellow workers. They need group support on their jobs, in their homes, and in their communities. Clubs, lodges, hobby groups, professional societies, unions, and all the other organizations are built around this need. Once group support is assured, people look for ways to be noticed as unique entities in the world. They want to be different as well as like the others.

Personal needs are those that make us demand treatment as individuals. This is what the youngster wants when she performs some childish trick and says, "Look at me! Look at me!" Some of these are needs for recognition and importance—being somebody others respect, having something others envy, standing out from the crowd. Just being *needed* is part of this satisfaction, as well as a feeling of having accomplished something worthwhile in life.

Social scientists and psychologists have tried to conceptualize the relationship that exists between human needs and motivation. One of the more famous of these conceptualizations was developed by the late psychologist Abraham Maslow and is depicted in Figure 3.

WHAT DOES THIS MEAN FOR SUPERVISORS?

Physical needs are no longer a main factor in getting people to work or produce more. If their jobs close out, government agencies take care of minimum wants, and social security dims the specter of poverty after retirement.

Even regular pay, benefits, and good conditions will not make people work harder. These are a normal part of the picture today and will only keep workers from being dissatisfied. They will stimulate enough work to get by, but they do not supply the *plus* factor that gets real action on the job.

What will make people feel like giving their best?

The Three Rs of Work Motivation

One able supervisor had this explanation for his success:

> I try to put everybody in business for himself. Each one of my people is in charge of some part of the job. I just hang around to

Figure 3. **Maslow's "Needs Hierarchy"**

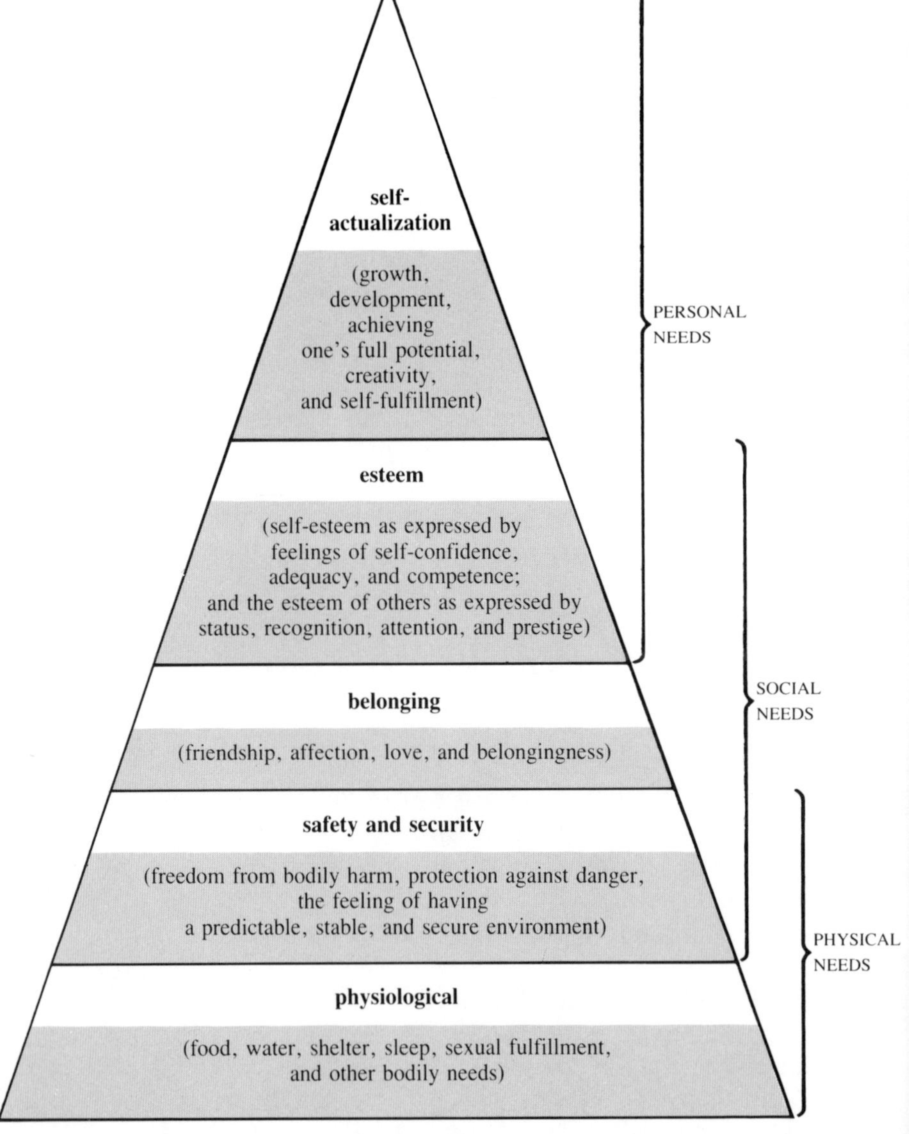

keep 'em out of trouble. When the work gets done, they get the credit. When it doesn't, they get the blame, and they know it. Mostly they blame themselves!

What people want from their jobs can be labeled the three Rs of work motivation; *responsibilities* they can handle, *results* they can show, and *recognition* for what they accomplish. In other words, they want to be respected as individuals who fill a needed and important place in the world. They want to be on their own as much as possible. The supervisor who breathes down their necks and gives an order for every move takes this satisfaction away from them. But the supervisor who gives them thorough training, points out the trouble spots, and then gets out of the way—this supervisor lets them develop pride and self-respect. And these lead to satisfaction of personal and social needs.

Employee Frustration

When people are not able to find recognition and respect at the workplace, they may look outside for their satisfactions. Proficiency in sports or hobbies can provide an outlet or activity in a club, church, or union group. Sometimes recognition at home as head of the household can meet the need. But the individual who is blocked in all directions may show what we call frustration symptoms. The supervisor will just have to cope with these.

Frustration shows up in various ways on the job. Chronic troublemaking and arguing may fall in this category. Childish behavior, complaining and blaming others for mistakes or failures, is another pattern. Sometimes, frustrated people just give up trying to get attention or recognition. They become early retirees who stay on the job. If the frustration is not too deeply ingrained, a good supervisor can use the three Rs of work motivation to bring the troubled workers around to normal behavior.

Employee Attitudes

People see things differently. They may be looking at the same factors or the same situation, but their feelings about what they see can vary widely. Each one puts a different frame around the picture, a frame made up of personal experiences. We call these differences *attitudes*, and they can complicate the life of a supervisor in a hundred ways. Every member of the work group carries around a private store of these feelings—pet likes and dislikes, slants, mind-sets, and prejudices. And supervisors have their own assortment to add to the collection.

For example, a young woman reports for a job under a quiet, steady, long-service supervisor. The newcomer has been raised in a family where all members were encouraged to voice their opinions. The family dinner table was an open forum and all the happenings of the household were subject to review. No subject was taboo and no viewpoint was sacred. The employee is bright, brash, and ready for action.

The supervisor had a very different upbringing. She was raised in a strict household where the chores were laid out for the youngsters and the parents made all the decisions. Younger members of the family were told what to think, how to act, and when to speak—if at all. The supervisor is a hard worker, knows her business, and tolerates no nonsense in the group.

The probability is strong that these two will have trouble understanding each other's viewpoints. There will be a personality clash. The responsibility, however, will still lie with the supervisor to work with the younger woman and tie her into the group.

Can attitudes be changed? Not by force or argument. People cannot be ordered to feel loyal to the company, for example, or to respect the supervisor. Patience, example, listening, and friendly discussion are the best approaches. But the more pressures that are brought to bear on an attitude, the more it tends to dig in and stay put.

THE SUM OF THE PARTS

Add up all these qualities and differences and we have a work force with a unique combination of abilities, needs, and feelings. The more supervisors take time to study their people and show interest in them as individuals, the closer they will move toward accepting leadership.

Individuals are the units supervisors use in building a team. Sometimes you may feel you are working with difficult and unstable elements, but the rewards are great when a productive work group with high morale can be developed. This is the challenge we will consider in the next section.

Check List . . . studying the people

1. People make the job go. They are worth study.

2. No two are alike. They are born different and experience is different.

3. Recognize differences among people and treat them as individuals.

4. Employees want to feel needed, run their jobs, show results, get credit.

5. Pay is important but only buys attendance—not support and hard work.

6. Best approach: give good training and put people on their own.

7. Some will not respond. Workers blocked from life goals may just put in time.

8. Attitudes will vary, too. People have different ways of looking at things.

9. Force and argument will not change feelings. Favorable experience may.

10. The more you understand your people, the better your chances of fitting them into the work situation.

5 · BUILDING THE TEAM

5 • Building the Team

A high-producing work unit is a group that pulls together to get the job done. Every supervisor would like to have this kind of action going on the job. The question is how to get it. To answer this we need a closer look at the work situation and the characteristics of groups themselves.

TEAM SPIRIT

Probably the best place for building team spirit is in a small shop or office. A trade contractor like a plumber, with a crew working under him, has a favorable climate right from the start. Jobs can be talked over at headquarters and on the way out in the truck. The whole operation is informal, and the lines of communication are short.

The supervisor in a large organization has more of a problem. Mass handling of people and materials means more set procedures and less personal contact. Jobs are specialized, so there is little chance for the group to work as a unit. Everybody gets the feeling of being lost in miles of machines, acres of desks, and reels of red tape. But team feeling can be generated even in this situation if companies and supervisors are willing to move toward a favorable setup.

GROUP IDENTITY

To build any kind of identity for groups in a large system, the small-and-separate principle needs to be followed. Groups should be built around a single work activity and their size kept down as much as possible. This allows for contact and exchange among members. Some effort should be made to mark off their area and equipment. They need a place of their own and a name of their own—Feeder Assembly No. 2, Office Services, or whatever will give them a banner to stand behind. It will help also if they have some kind of table or flat piece of equipment to meet around and a time like coffee or lunch to get together. Finally, they need to have demands made on them as a group—a schedule for the day or week: "Here's what we need from your outfit. Can you deliver?" Add to this a leader who knows the business, and the signs are favorable for good morale and productivity. There are other ways to warm up the cold corporate climate but this one has some built-in advantages.

DISAFFECTION

The alternative is what we often have now in large mass-production operations: a hostility barrier between workers and supervisors, a lack of interest in company success, and a nagging series of grievances, slowdowns, walkouts, and demands.

Small businesses have fewer of these problems. They seem to be able to make people feel at home on the job—and needed. With good planning and the right tools, the work gets done and the group finds satisfaction in doing it.

WORK PATTERNS

As much flexibility as possible is needed in this kind of close-team operation. Some studies of people on the job show that many find straight routine deadening. They may become troublemakers or find relief by getting into outside activities. Repetitive work fails to challenge them as mature, independent adults, and they feel dissatisfied. Companies have been told that as long as they offer monotonous jobs, they can expect morale problems.

All this is only partly true. Many employees find security in familiar routines and resist too much challenge. They will go along with moving from one routine to another, but they want to feel they are on firm and friendly ground.

For both these groups, the informal methods of a small work team can be a happy middle ground. The members can talk over the jobs for the day and move into them with some degree of flexibility. As the work goes along, they can shift naturally from one part of the operation to another. Change and movement can make the routines tolerable for some and still comfortable for the others.

AUTOMATION

Small-group procedures provide more change of pace for workers, but automation is still in order for long-run production. If the firm's business outlook warrants the investment, equipment should be installed to take over monotonous parts of the work. Eternal repetition of one operation can make a mechanoid out of any man or woman. The normal routines left over after the machines get through will still require the flexibility and informality of small-group operation.

There is no doubt that the work situation can have its effect on team spirit and productivity. The size of the unit, the methods used, the layout, location, and leadership provided—all these can influence the group's general attitude.

Another factor is the nature of the group itself and the forces within it that work on each other. In some ways groups are like individuals. They are all different and tend to have characteristics and personalities of their own.

THE MAKEUP OF GROUPS

A work team starts out as a plain body of people brought together by the chance of being hired into the same outfit. As soon as the group assembles, all the pulls and tugs of human relationships begin to operate. These can tear it apart into cliques or draw it together into a cooperative, productive unit. To build a team, supervisors need to understand something about these forces and how they work.

The Pecking Order

When any number of people come together, a pecking order is soon established. This is an informal alignment based on the status and authority some members hold over others. The existence of a pecking order was detected long ago by students of group behavior. It is modeled, of course, after the barnyard scene, where the biggest bird establishes the right to peck all the other chickens in the flock and so on down the line. The youngest or weakest pullet gets pecked by everyone else. As newcomers enter the picture, they are tried and tested until a new order is worked out.

The same pattern develops in a group of people. Highest place in the pecking order goes to the ones who have what students of street gangs call Mind, Mouth, and Muscle. The best mix of these for each group will be different, depending on the background of the members. *Mind* usually draws respect in every situation. The top of the pecking order in a work group may be an unofficial leader, a union steward, or the supervisor, who carries the added weight of his or her official position.

Stars, Pairs, and Isolates

Another force at work in a group is made up of the attractions and rejections that continually occur among its members. One individual may be favored by all the others and constitute a kind of star around which the members revolve. This person may or may not be at the top of the pecking order, but his or her status, influence, or special qualities draw all the others closer. Such a person's opinions and example will carry weight and are factors the supervisor will have to reckon with.

A group may not boast a star, but it certainly will have pairs or trios of members who tend to hang together. These alliances are formed for various reasons but are encouraged by close proximity on the job. Pairs or trios seek each other out, eat together, and talk over whatever is on their minds. They constitute subgroups within the larger body. This teaming up is as natural as boys and girls finding "best friends" in the neighborhood. Supervisors can simply recognize it as a condition of group life to which they must accommodate.

Sometimes individuals come into a group but are not accepted into full membership. These are isolates from the main body. Rejection may come from their failure to accept the group's standards of work or behavior. They may challenge the pecking order and lose out. In some cases, they may prefer to be different and alone. The existence of isolates can complicate the job of building a team. The best approach is not to force the issue but to let matters work themselves out gradually.

Sometimes the isolates adapt slowly to the group or are accepted finally as different but familiar.

TRANSFORMATION OF THE GROUP

There are signs that tell when strong bonds have been established. Free exchange of ideas and opinions prevails among the members. They naturally help each other, support each other, cover for each other. When they reach the work location, members feel they are coming into a place where they are known and wanted. They can exchange friendly insults, but they make common front against outsiders. For many employees, the main satisfaction they get from their work is association with the group. They have pride in the team and resist leaving it even for better opportunities.

With all these values and benefits, a group still may not be a highly productive unit or have a favorable attitude toward the supervisor or the company. Certain other elements have to be brought into the picture to create a supportive attitude toward the establishment.

Teamwork

If we set up a scale to indicate the amount of work interest that could exist in a group, we would probably have a range from enthusiasm at the top to apathy or hostility at the bottom. Somewhere in between would be a so-so, it's-a-job attitude. What will influence a team to go at its work with a high level of interest and enthusiasm?

First, the group needs to feel that the general company climate is a fair and friendly one, not cold and corporate. Employees must believe they can get a fair shake from management. They may not have everything their way, but they must know they will not get pushed around or brushed off.

Second, the group members must see that the supervisor who represents management is also on their side. And the supervisor must know what their side looks like, treat members of the team as individuals, and make efforts to understand them.

Third, the supervisor must use a group approach in handling the work. This involves listening to everybody's ideas and drawing them in on the planning. When a piece of equipment breaks down or a problem comes up, everybody gets into the act. The supervisor works out changes with the team and lets the team know what is coming before it happens.

Fourth, the supervisor must be accepted into the team as part of the operation, and not seen as an outsider imposing controls on the members. Management may even let the group help select the supervisor by allowing employees to nominate a few candidates, with the final decision reserved to those in charge.

Given these conditions, a healthy, highly productive work unit is likely to result.

The Kickoff

Up to this point in our discussion, as a supervisor you have sized up your responsibilities, planned your approach, organized the work, studied your people, and built the team. Now you are ready for the kickoff—the job gets under way, and you head out onto the floor. Your goal is to keep the work moving under any and all conditions—and the conditions will keep changing. New processes, new people, new equipment, and new orders from above will keep coming into the picture.

The next section will describe adjustments the supervisor will be required to make to keep up with these demands, plus the hundred and one other problems of running the job.

Check List . . .
building the team

1. How can you build a productive work unit that pulls together?

2. First, give the group identity—a name and place of its own.

3. Add good leadership and a production goal.

4. Allow for flexibility—changing around on the jobs.

5. Reduce monotony factors.

6. Recognize the pecking order and the pulls and tugs of relationships.

7. Look for signs that the group has become a team—likes to be together.

8. Add a fair and friendly company climate.

9. Play straight and allow open discussion of work and problems.

10. Your chances will then be good that a healthy, productive work team will result.

6 · DIRECTING THE OPERATION

6 • Directing the Operation

One foreman said, "My job is like driving a 20-mule team. Every morning I back the critters into the harness, get the rig rolling, keep the whip cracking, and bring the load in on time." That kind of description might give an idea of this foreman's general approach to his duties. If, on the other hand, he had applied the lessons we have been over up to now, the "critters" could pretty well have brought the load in by themselves. What we have covered to this point is the make-ready for supervision. The next step is the operation itself and the process of running it smoothly.

TIME-USE PATTERNS

Several studies have been made of front-line managers at work. The results show a general time-use pattern like this:

Supervisory Task	*Time-use %*
Planning and Scheduling	15
Assigning Jobs	10
Checking Work	20
Coaching and Training	20
Handling Problems	10
Observing and Improving	5
Meetings and Telephone	5
Record Keeping	15

This pattern will vary, of course, with the kind of work and the organization involved. Travel time would be a factor in field operations. At many locations the supervisors do part of the work themselves and have less time for observing and checking. In some other places, the planning, training, and record keeping are taken out of their hands by staff people.

The studies also show that supervisors spend much of their time in listening and talking—part with their own people and part with outsiders. The contacts are short, usually five minutes or less. And, except for records and reports, supervisors are found to do little reading on the job.

Most of their activities are straight work direction with plenty of back-and-forth discussion. The main problems that take up supervisory time can be reviewed by moving through a typical day at a work location.

THE STARTUP

Supervisors generally get to the job early to check things over. They study the orders for the day, clear up any problems, and start laying out the work. When employees come in, supervisors set up the schedule and try to get everybody at work as quickly as possible.

Absenteeism

Most supervisors agree their biggest headaches are caused by late and absent workers. Employees may wait till the last minute to call in sick. Others simply do not come in at all. Supervisors are forced to cover the jobs any way they can by transferring people around or by bringing in replacements at extra cost.

Illness, real or imagined, is the reason for 75 percent of absence. The other 25 percent comes from a variety of causes, such as family problems, personal business, and a negative attitude toward the job. We can only guess at how much of a factor this negative attitude may be. Much of it disappears as, and if, workers move up the ladder. Responsible owners and managers themselves are seldom absent. The question is how much responsibility can be put into every employee's job.

Supervisors can go a long way by demonstrating how the work goes better when every individual is present. This cannot be faked, however; an absence has to cause a real difficulty for the supervisor in meeting work demands. Otherwise, any excuse will do to incline the worker toward staying away from his post. One analyst put it as simply as this:

A headache + being needed on the job = attendance
A headache + not being needed = absence

How to Reduce Absenteeism

Like death and taxes, some absences will always be with us, but supervisors can hold the rate down by following a few simple procedures:

Talk about absences with the group. Do not dwell on the cost to the company—emphasize instead the need for a full crew to get the work out. Point out the handicaps for the rest of the team when one of the group is out. If the group is young, mention the fact that an attendance record, good or bad, stays with an employee from year to year and job to job. Show why absences make problems for you as the supervisor and why you want to hold them down. But state also that the work will be performed without question when an absence is necessary. You want no one to come in when he or she is sick or has real problems at home. Review the rules covering absenteeism with the group.

Follow up on absences regularly. Show concern over any accident or illness and mean it. People have a right to believe their welfare is more important than keeping equipment running or getting the work out. They are also less inclined to take advantage of a supervisor who is on their side and plays straight.

When a case of deliberate absenteeism is uncovered, state the facts privately in plain terms to the offender. Give a full hearing but point out that continuing absence by one member is unfair to the rest of the group. Use the same approach to an employee whose record, even for justifiable reasons, is running higher than can be tolerated. Administer an oral warning and make a note of the case.

If absenteeism continues, issue a written warning, and, if no improvement is made, take positive action—suspension or dismissal, as company policy requires. Let the rest of the group know what was done and why.

The important factor in this procedure is regular attention to absences day in and day out. Workers try to live up to the supervisor's expectations if administration is consistent. With everybody accounted for, the supervisor can move on to the next problem, getting production underway.

WORK ASSIGNMENTS

In some operations, the startup is automatic. People know their duties and go about them without special orders. Even in routine situations, however, there are times when a change has to be made and different signals given. In still other kinds of work, new orders or requests come in every day and require the supervisor to state who will handle which assignments.

The Go Principle

Pilots and astronauts proceed on the basis that no trip starts until all signals are *go*. This is a good practice to follow any time in starting people out on a project. Employees are entitled to enough information to do the job right. They need to know what they can expect and what is expected of them. Let's see what happens when the *go* system is not followed.

A busy supervisor calls the supply room. He issues orders for a load of rods to be sent to Number 5 and delivered to Joe. He hangs up and departs. Unless the signals were clear from previous experience, the employee receiving the order has these questions to answer: Which rods? How many in a load? How soon? Where and what is Number 5? Should delivery be made if Joe is not there? In this case, with the supervisor gone, a call back will not clear up these questions.

The Two-Way Review

But being clear also saves time! The *go* principle calls for a two-way review of all steps in a project. Even an experienced worker can stand checking to make sure he or she knows what is wanted. If everybody in the outfit understands and follows this system, there will be no resentment when an assignment is covered in detail.

Of course, the best way to get understanding by all concerned with a project is to talk over the plan with the whole group. This approach is fine when major projects are being undertaken but cannot be justified under normal conditions. Most of the time, orders are routine or the situation cannot wait for lengthy discussion.

How to Give Orders

There is a certain amount of resistance to authority in the best of people, and supervisors gain no advantage by aggravating the feeling. Favorable results are usually obtained by stating orders in the form of questions or requests. Instead of blasting out a command, the smart supervisor gives directions like this: ''Will you clean up around Number 2, Meg? The porter is off sick today.'' This has three things going for it that are likely to get cooperation. First, it is a request, not a demand. Second, the employee's name is used, which gives a personal rather than an official tone. And third, a reason is given which answers the employee's unspoken question, ''Why me?''

A supervisor may have to give a direct order if such requests are ignored, but direct orders should be given as a last resort. The best rule is to avoid arbitrary action as much as possible. Bossing with a capital B increases the hostility between management and worker, which is enough of a problem as it is.

BEST FOOT FORWARD

Part of the day's work for the supervisor is to break in new people. Too many times, though, responsibility for this part of the job is abdicated. The newcomer gets a fast handshake and is turned over to another worker for training and general orientation. It may be necessary to let a senior employee do the training, but dropping all responsibility is not good practice. When this happens, it says that the boss does not consider the new employee or the job to be very important.

Let's look at it this way. This is the first chance the supervisor has to establish a sound working relationship with the employee. If the supervisor fails to do so, there will be others who will take over the job. All the loaf artists and sea lawyers in the area will be glad to show the new man or woman their way of sidestepping duties. The employee soon begins to turn for counsel to these questionable advisers, or to the steward if a union is involved.

Orientation

Procedures may vary for breaking in new people, but they should include these points somewhere along the line:

Make newcomers welcome, show them around, introduce them to the group.

Talk over the personal matters they will wonder about, such as hours of work, where to report, location of facilities, food arrangements, and how and when they will be paid.

Review each job and the way it ties in with other operations. Emphasize the need for good workers in those positions. Talk over the general plan for orientation and training so they know what to expect.

If there is time, invite them to walk around a while and observe what goes on. Let them get the feel of the place. Warn them about hazards, if any exist in the area.

Review the rules and company benefits. If there is a union agreement, tell them about it. Answer questions and leave the way open for them to come back with any other points they think of later.

Start the training. If you use a senior worker to help on this, make sure an organized plan is followed so the new worker will get a solid foundation. Mastery of the job will bring a feeling of real worth and confidence.

Keep in contact after the new worker starts handling the work alone. Check progress, answer questions, show interest.

THE TRAINING PROCESS

Plain and unskilled work can be taught by the old tell-show-and-do method. *Tell* new workers what their job is; *show* them how to do it; then have them *do* it while they are watched and corrected. Sorting mail, cleaning windows, and other routine chores can be handled this way without going into a complicated training procedure. Anything beyond this, however, requires a task analysis or job breakdown along with a training plan. An *analysis* is an in-depth study which includes details of the knowledge and skills required for the job. This process requires special background on the part of the analyst and is not normally handled by the supervisor. The *breakdown*, on the other hand, is a simple step-by-step listing of the moves made in doing a piece of work. Along with every step, safety hints and short cuts can be added to make the job run smoothly. Supervisors in all kinds of work can prepare job breakdowns for procedures ranging from packing a pump in a plant to serving a customer in a retail establishment. An example on the home front would be an orderly procedure for members of the family to follow in changing a tire.

The Training Plan

Whether the supervisor handles the instruction personally or directs a senior worker to carry it out, a training plan should be followed. For new employees with previous experience, the training plan can be less detailed, but these employees will still need to know the standards and practices in effect at the new location. For inexperienced workers, supervisors must go through the steps at a slower pace. The plan for supervisors outlined here will help them to give newcomers a solid understanding of their jobs:

First, know the job thoroughly yourself. Trainers cannot give clear explanations unless they have been through all the steps themselves.

Second, have the training setup ready, with the needed tools and supplies and the operating manuals or job breakdown sheets handy.

Third, talk over the whole operation to give new employees a general picture of what the job is about. Tell them they are not under any pressure; you expect them to take a while to get the knack. Find out about past experience and special characteristics like left-handedness or color-blindness.

Fourth, go through the job one step at a time. Show how each step is performed and explain it. Have them follow on the breakdown sheet.

Fifth, have them go through the step-by-step procedure, explaining what they are doing as they go along. Be sure they repeat any key points listed for each step covered. Make any corrections needed and answer questions. Have them repeat the operation until you see they understand. Then move on to the next part of the job and proceed as before. Finally, tie the steps together and have them covered in series.

Sixth, put them on their own. Give them the standards in time and quality that they will be expected to meet and tell them where to check if they need help. Taper off on close supervision.

The Alternative

Supervisors are busy people and sometimes feel they can save time by using hit-or-miss training procedures. Generally, this costs them time and production in the long run. Shoddy workmanship, disregard for safety requirements, and failure to meet standards are more often found where instruction has been given in bits and pieces.

COACHING ON THE JOB

With basic training covered, the supervisor is free to move around and give help where needed. The key word here is *help*—not criticism. Some supervisors bear down on a work group like a cruiser moving into battle action. Everybody gets braced for the attack. Good coaches, on the other hand, work quietly and make their points by raising questions and offering suggestions. They check to see if the right tools and supplies are on hand, ask how the job is going, give a few pointers, and move along. If there are any problems, they listen carefully and work them out.

Good coaching is an art. Here are a few techniques that usually pay off in better production and higher morale:

Establish a good working relationship from the start. Handle contacts in a way that makes people on the job like to have you come around.

Be available to workers so they can touch base from time to time. When they do, give them support, ask about the work, draw them out.

Show confidence in their ability. Put this into practice; give them responsibility and put them on their own as much as possible.

Go out of the way to make contacts with them. Put a reminder on the calendar if you are apt to forget.

When contacts are made, try to include some added bit of instruction if needed. It is not necessary to preach to experienced workers; instead, get their ideas on any question that comes up.

When corrections are needed, make them without delay. Your manner should be matter-of-fact and businesslike. Do not nag about an error; make your point and drop the subject.

Listen actively and encourage workers to talk. Get them to use you as a sounding board for thinking things through. Let them come up with the answers.

Use on-the-job meetings with the group as coaching sessions. Do some planning and problem solving. Get everybody into the act.

Operate like a coach on the playing field. Work to improve performance, not to catch errors. Allow workers the freedom to make mistakes, when hazards are not involved, and to learn from them.

When differences of opinion come up, restate the workers' ideas and check to see if you have them right. Accept what you can, and give them your own thinking. If there is a difference in methods and there are no risks, let them try their own systems to see how they work.

OBSERVATION TRIPS

Coaching is not the only reason for making trips around the work area. Effective supervisors are sharp observers, but they also look with a purpose. Random visits are better than no visits at all, but the best results come when checks are made on one kind of problem at a time. On one trip you might concentrate on security matters—protection against pilferage and loss. At other times look for safety, morale, housekeeping, waste, methods improvement, tools and equipment, maintenance, job records, or other items.

The value of this one-track approach is that coverage is more thorough. Problems are seen that might well be overlooked on a general walk-through, and notes can be made for needed action. A good idea is to set up a reminder system on the calendar for scheduling each kind of observation.

Job Safety

"Safety Is No Accident." This is a familiar slogan to safety experts, and it means just what it says. Safety is Prevention! The way to proceed is to correct the trouble before a disaster happens.

Supervisors are called on to talk safety, practice safety, and check for safety at every turn. Dangers can come from any direction and are present in what seems to be the most risk-free situation in the world.

Every job has its own safety factors to consider. Even in office areas there are drawers left open, wires to trip over, heavy objects stored on high shelves, paper cutters, and high-speed equipment. In the stock room there are lifting problems and step ladders to climb. No area is free from hazard.

A listing of safe procedures to cover all work situations would be endless. Some common problems and precautions are listed here for supervisors' guidance in giving appropriate warnings to their people.

Before starting equipment, know what is going to happen and know how to stop it. Ask if in doubt.

Before starting to move an object, have a place ready for setting it down.

Lift with the back straight and knees flexed, not with the body in a bent position.

Keep fingers away from moving machinery. Do not adjust or lubricate machines in operation.

Avoid cuts from sharp edges—including paper. Avoid picking up broken glass or metal chips with bare hands.

Use tools that are right for the purpose—wrenches that fit and cutting tools that are sharp.

Clean up or cover all spillage. Spills are dangerous.

Do not leave standing ladders unattended when conditions can cause sliding. Set base and head of ladders firmly.

Use appropriate goggles around grinding wheels and in all areas where flying particles are present.

Use appropriate ear covers in all areas where noise is loud and penetrating. Hearing can be lost.

Use appropriate masks to cover mouth and nostrils in all areas where paint and chemical fumes are heavy and clinging.

Do not leave machines running when not in a position to check and control the operation.

When around moving equipment, watch loose clothing and avoid using rags.

Never look directly without protection at the blaze of a welding tool.

Take time to learn all hazards in an area and observe proper precautions.

Use hard hats at all construction locations and in plants as required.

Respect all safety tags, notices, and barriers. Check with responsible people before bypassing regulations.

When, despite all precautions, an accident does occur, the supervisor is expected to make a complete record including the who, what, when, where, and why, retaining one copy and sending others as required by the organization. Work-induced illnesses should also be covered by record.

Records and Reports

Getting the work out is only part of the picture. Records need to be kept to show what happened along the way. Supervisors who let paperwork slide can soon get a reputation for doing only half the job. Here are three good reasons for completing reports on time and in detail:

Records on production and operating problems are the only basis management has for sizing up the whole operation and for planning ahead. The front-line supervisor is the one who can best see what goes on. The rest of the organization relies on these reports to help reach the right decisions.

Supervisors need records for their own planning and to meet any questions that come up later. Grievance cases, tax and accident investigations, checks on personnel, and special surveys may require a search back in the files for the facts. The wise supervisor has the information on tap when needed.

In smaller operations supervisors may be held accountable for most of the record keeping. In larger ones they have all the additional paperwork required by systems, personnel, and technical people as well as by their own line organizations.

Two kinds of records need to be considered. There are the routine kind that are entered on the books every day: time reports, production, scrap, supplies requisitioned, and others. Then there are special matters that need to be noted: a problem with another supervisor, a safety hazard uncovered, a suggestion for improving the job, and so on. The trick on these individual items is to make notes at the time so details are not lost. Writing them down takes a load off the memory.

THE WINDUP

At the end of the day supervisors have some cleanup work to do. They check to see that all records are complete and reports are on the way. If another shift is coming on, they pass along needed information to the next group leader. They look over the calendar to see what is scheduled for the time ahead and lay out general plans. They make a final trip through the location to check on conditions and security. And the supervisor is the last one out.

Check List... directing the operation

1. Get to the job early. Lay out the work.

2. Start operations without delay. Make clear assignments.

3. Follow up on absences. Show workers they are needed.

4. Give orders without unnecessary display of authority.

5. Establish favorable relations with new employees. Plan their training.

6. Coach people on the job. Help rather than criticize. Solve problems.

7. Make trips through the work area. Look for one kind of problem at a time.

8. Concentrate on safety. Every situation offers hazards.

9. Keep records and reports up to date.

10. Make a final check and be the last one out.

7 · KEEPING THE LINES OPEN

7 • Keeping the Lines Open

Supervisors spend most of their time communicating—some say as much as 90 percent. Communication is the name of the game—the way supervisors get their work accomplished. Successful group leaders need to be Signal Specialists, First Class.

UP, DOWN, AND SIDEWAYS

In any organization the flow of information moves in at least three directions: up from workers to higher levels, down from management to the front line, and across from one group to another to keep the whole operation geared together. The supervisor is the one in the middle who sees that the word gets through. When the flow is blocked by a nontalking group leader, the trouble starts. Communication is the lifeblood of any organization, and if it is not kept moving through clear channels, unhealthy conditions set in. One sign of a blockage is the bypass of a supervisor by the workers—they start dealing directly with higher levels. Another sign is the reverse situation—the manager goes around the supervisor to contact people on the job.

The Grapevine

Still another mark of poor signaling is a heavy run of rumors. Usually a clear report of the facts will render the grapevine inactive. The best way is to state the case before the rumor starts, but this is not always possible. Sometimes there are good reasons for holding back, and in other cases stories may begin that could not be anticipated. Where the facts can be told, supervisors should step in promptly with the truth.

On these occasions it is just as well not to repeat the rumor in the process of putting it down. Repetition tends to prolong its life even while it is being disproved.

When there are good reasons for not telling everything, state the reasons but not the facts. Be open about it. Say the subject is still confidential or that all the plans have not been worked out. Most workers understand, for example, that, when changes are being made, the people directly involved have to be notified first. Others are willing to wait their turns.

Information generally falls under one of three headings. First, what individuals *must* know to get their work done. Second, what they *should* know because it will affect them one way or another. And third, what they *would like to* know because they are interested. Healthy curiosity should not be suppressed. It is a sign of concern and far better than a hostile or indifferent attitude toward the whole enterprise. So far as possible, information should be provided to satisfy all three levels of need.

RULES FOR GOOD COMMUNICATION

Correct signaling is a complex process, and the list of do's and don'ts would be endless if we tried to cover all points. The main ones are these:

Communication requires a completed circuit. Talking and writing, by themselves, are not communications. Listening or reading with understanding is required at the other end to make them effective. The best way to make sure that information has been received as intended is to ask for feedback. What did the receiver understand by what was said?

A communication has the best chance of getting through if it is adjusted to fit the people on the receiving end. A new piece of equipment, for example, would be explained in operating terms to the people on the job and in cost and production terms to the manager. A visiting group from a nearby school would get still a different explanation.

Words are not the only tools for communicating. Everything we do conveys a message: looks, manner, tone, gestures. Sometimes words themselves get in the way of understanding when they carry different meanings for the parties involved. Even silence tells a story when a statement is expected. An upper-level manager, for instance, who puffs on a cigar or cigarette while walking through a no-smoking area leaves a trail of communication behind without saying a word.

A little planning helps to make the message come through with best effect. The supervisor who has an interview scheduled with an employee gets better results by taking a few minutes to work out an approach ahead of time. A comment being passed around in companies today points up the need for preparation: "I know you believe you understand what you think I said, but what you don't know is that what you heard is not what I meant."

Effective speaking or writing usually holds to the ABC pattern. First, accuracy: get the facts straight. Second, brevity: say only what's needed. Third, clarity: make it easy to understand.

With these rules in mind, supervisors have a better chance of avoiding all the rework, mistakes, waste, confusion, and arguments that come from incomplete and garbled communications on the job. The time and money saved would be considerable if we also included the strikes, slowdowns, turnover, and absenteeism that often result from faulty signaling.

ONE-TO-ONE COMMUNICATIONS

Supervisors spend most of their time in contacts with one individual at a time. They give assignments, hold interviews, make phone calls, and talk with staff people or managers. All of these call for special techniques which should be mentioned.

Clear Assignments

We have already discussed part of this topic in an earlier section. Some guidelines can be added here to help on this basic activity. Probably the best recipe is provided by the 5 W's used in newspaper writing. These are *who*, *what*, *when*, *where*, and *why*, with *how* added for good measure. Once these questions are answered in giving instructions, you can feel you have covered all necessary points.

Who is to carry out the assignment? This will make a difference in the terms used to explain it. A new or untried employee will require extra information. If more than one is involved in working on a project, the employee in charge should be designated.

What is to be done? This should be stated in clear language. If there is any possibility of confusion on some of the terms, repeat the assignment using different words. You will need to think through the project yourself before you can say definitely what it is you want. If you have not yet worked this out, the assignment should be labeled an exploratory one to get the facts. This will avoid extra work and bother for the people trying to do the job.

When is the assignment to be carried out? This should cover the time for starting the work, dates for reporting progress, and the deadline for completion. If other work is going on at the same time, priorities should be established. The use of ASAP (as soon as possible) is confusing and should be avoided.

Where is the work to be done? This may seem unnecessary if there is a regular location for an activity. Source of materials and information should be provided and authority to request them as needed.

Why is always important. Blind obedience to an order is proper only in an emergency. At other times, people have a right to know the purpose. They can give intelligent cooperation in reaching the goal. Do not just ask for a hole to be dug; state what the hole is for.

How covers the methods for doing the job—what steps to take, what to look out for, what to do first. With new employees these should be checked over carefully. Experienced people can be left pretty much on their own.

Of all these suggestions, one should be underscored for supervisors. *Think through an assignment before passing it on.* There are few experiences more frustrating than trying to carry out directions from bosses who are not sure themselves what they want.

Interviews

All meetings between two people are not interviews. Casual contacts are not in this category, and neither are one-way lectures where the supervisor calls in an employee for a warning or reprimand. An interview requires an exchange of facts and feelings with a definite purpose in mind. When a decision is to be reached that involves both parties, a discussion is in order.

One example, of course is the familiar hiring interview. The mistake many supervisors make in this situation is to do most of the talking. Their real objective should be to draw out the applicant. Other instances would be interviews about poor work performance, absenteeism or general misconduct around the premises. Complaints, suggestions, and personal problems are all matters best dealt with by supervisors who listen more than they talk.

Let's take an absence case as a sample. An employee has a record of frequent days off the job. There may or may not be justifiable reasons, but the supervisor believes that an interview is called for. The supervisor's part of the exchange is to state the facts, including the general absence standards to be met, and then to put the problem directly in the employee's lap: "Here's where you stand, Carol. What do you plan to do about it?" From this point on the supervisor listens and questions until the absentee comes up with an acceptably corrective program. This approach is much more likely to get results than a lecture and threats.

Many a supervisor has been heard to say, "I don't understand this man. I've talked and talked and he still comes up with a bad record." The difficulty may be that the supervisor has never placed the responsibility on the employee and let the individual find the answers.

The Process of Listening

Effective listening is the simple process of paying such close attention to another individual that he feels impelled to open up and keep talking. When the flow of words runs dry, the pump can be primed by asking a question. All of us like to be listened to and feel favorable toward the people who do the listening. Able salesmen and managers have used this approach for years. What it shows is respect for the other person's ideas and experiences.

Guide to Good Listening

Here are some steps to follow in conducting a good listening session.

A start is made when one of the parties states the reason for wanting an interview. A time is set, and the supervisor clears the decks for active listening. The best situation is one where there will be no interruptions. If the supervisor's desk is the only location available, distractions should be screened out as much as possible.

As supervisor, your opening question or statement can get the ball rolling. This would restate the reason given earlier for scheduling an interview. An example might be, "You said you were thinking of quitting, Jack. Do you want to tell me about it?" Or, you might give your own purpose: "I called you in, Jack, because your work has been falling off and we need to talk it over. What's the problem as you see it."

You as supervisor should register a listening attitude, sitting up and leaning forward, maintaining eye contact without staring, showing interest in what is said, and staying calm no matter how excited or abusive the employee becomes. Most of all, you should screen out interruptions and stick to the business at hand.

You should try to make no comments that will lead to an argument. Answer questions of fact, such as "How much pay would I have coming if I left now?" Avoid replies to questions of opinion such as, "Nobody can get along with that character, can they?" Or, "This is a real cheap outfit, isn't it?" Answers can be neutral, as, "I'm interested in how you feel about it, Jack." The object is to keep the employee feeling free to talk, not to draw him or her into a 'tis-'tain't argument.

Put in remarks or questions from time to time to move the discussion along. These can be simple expressions like "uh-huh," "I see," "oh," "well," or others that signal to the employee that he or she is being tuned in and received. Use questions to draw out more information. "What happened then?" "How did you feel about that?" "Did you report this to anyone?"

Occasionally summarize what the employee has covered: "Now, as I understand it, Jack, this happened twice, and you did what you could but got no satisfaction. As you see it now, quitting is the best answer." This assures the employee that you were listening and allows an opportunity to correct wrong impressions. It also helps the employee review the situation and primes him or her to talk further.

When all the facts and feelings have been stated, put the key question: "What do you plan to do?," or "How will you handle this?" These are open-end questions which require the employee to do the thinking and deciding. It is best to avoid closed-end questions, such as, "Don't you think if you cooperated more, you could get along better?" Or, "If you got up earlier, you could get here on time, couldn't you?" These are closed-end because you are trying to force the employee into a "yes" answer. Questions like this are disguised ways of preaching and lecturing. The real action comes when the employee is the one who decides to change.

Finally, summarize the steps the employee is now committed to take. Make notes on any part you have agreed to play—information to get or promises to fill. If there are still some points to cover, set a time for continuing the discussion.

What happens if the employee is not a talker or proves to be just as good a listener as the supervisor? Will the whole interview bog down? Not usually. If there is really something on the employee's mind, it will come out. All that is needed is encouragement.

Telephone Procedures

Telephone procedure is so simple it seems hardly worth mentioning. We still have abuses, though, and a few words may help.

First, a phone call is not the time for experimenting with sound pickup from different angles. Talk straight into the mouthpiece without shouting or muttering. Use a normal conversational tone.

Second, keep business calls on the brief side. Allow for break periods if a succession of calls is being made. The instrument is normally meant for two-way traffic.

Third, remember that tone and inflection have to take the place of all gestures and expressions in getting your point across. Voices pitched low usually come over better than high, grating ones. Good telephone presence can be developed with practice.

THE CALL TO ORDER

Most of the time front-line supervisors hold their meetings right on the job. They call the group together at the desk or bench or at the tailgate of a truck when the crew is out in the field. Meetings have different purposes: to talk over plans and methods, pass along instructions and information, work out job problems, or just to bring feelings and complaints out in the open.

Supervisors have the same responsibilities in these meetings that they have in holding interviews, plus a few extras because a group is involved. First, they must think through in advance what it is they want to accomplish. Second, they must get the meeting started by stating what it's about and giving all the facts. Third, they should try to keep the discussion on target and get the group to open up. And last, they wind up the session and review what has been decided.

The Meeting Climate

The climate of the meeting is important. Workers are willing to talk if what they say is listened to and respected. They like an honest, open discussion in which they know the plan and purpose from the start. If the object is to tell them about a new policy or procedure which has already been established, they know they can ask questions but cannot make changes. If an exploratory or attitude-airing session is planned, say so and point out that no final action or conclusions will be reached. As supervisor you are charged with setting the ground rules under which discussion will be held. You position the group at the start.

Some companies follow a regular plan for on-the-job information meetings. They are scheduled once a month or once a week and are intended to bring out a two-way flow of ideas. You pass along any information you have about the job and the company, and the workers raise questions, make requests, offer suggestions, and register complaints. These regular meetings are in addition to problem-solving sessions.

What to Avoid

There are a few warnings to keep in mind for running a successful meeting. If you are not prepared for the session, you will do best not to hold it at all. Aimless, unplanned gatherings are what give meetings a bad name. Avoid reading long documents to the group. Draw the main points out of the material, and pass them along as a summary list. Do not take up the group's time on matters that involve only one member. Meet with her or him separately. And finally, when discussion runs out, pull together what has been covered and adjourn. If a further session is needed, schedule it.

PUBLIC SPEAKING

Retirement parties, award dinners, open houses—all supervisors face times when they are called on to say a few words. The simplest recipe for these occasions is an old familiar one: Stand up! Speak up! Shut up! Remember, audiences like speakers who can be heard clearly and who keep their talks short.

The best way to avoid nervousness is to be prepared. With the main points of your talk in mind, you can relax and enjoy the affair. When the introduction is made, step up confidently. Take a minute to look around at different parts of the group, nod, and acknowledge the introduction. Open with a statement on why you are speaking to this particular group at this time on this subject. In other words, position the audience. Do not try any stories unless three conditions are met: (1) You are good at telling them; (2) They can be told without apology; and (3) They tie in with the subject.

Have closing remarks ready at hand. State them and sit down. No "thank you" is needed if the talk has been brief. The last lines of the Toastmaster's Prayer can serve as a reminder:

Lord, fill my mouth with worthwhile stuff
and nudge me when I've said enough.

PAPER WORK

When communications are official or needed for the record, the written form is preferred. These include notices for posting as well as memos and special papers. Examples would include reports on accidents, disciplinary actions, grievances, production problems, and the like. Supervisors are occasionally asked to make studies for management, and these need to be pulled together in clear and readable form.

A good plan is to put down everything needed to tell the complete story and then sort it out in organized form. At the start, state the subject and fill in all the who-what-when-where-why facts. If a conclusion or recommendation is in order, give reasons for the position taken. Be sure all material is dated and signed. If the report is a long one, put a short summary at the front along with your recommendation. This saves time for the manager who reviews it. The manager can read the rest if he or she wants all the details.

REPORTS

Records and reports are the basis for management planning. Supervisors contribute to the process by keeping track of progress and performance on their jobs and reporting up the line. The information is needed by managers to correct problems and make necessary changes. The next section shows how these reports are used and emphasizes the supervisor's role as a front-line controller.

Check List... keeping the lines open

1. Remember, supervisors are key communicators in the organization.

2. Keep information moving down from management, up from workers, and across to other groups.

3. Watch ABC's of communication. Be accurate, brief, and clear.

4. Cover all points in making assignments. Check for understanding.

5. Do more listening than talking in interviews. Make free use of questions.

6. Plan ahead for meetings. State purpose and keep discussion on target.

7. In giving talks, speak up clearly and close early.

8. Use normal tone in telephoning. Hold business calls to brief side.

9. Reports are important for management planning. Get facts organized before writing.

10. Keep in mind that every look, tone, and gesture communicates. Even silence tells a story.

8 · CHECKING RESULTS

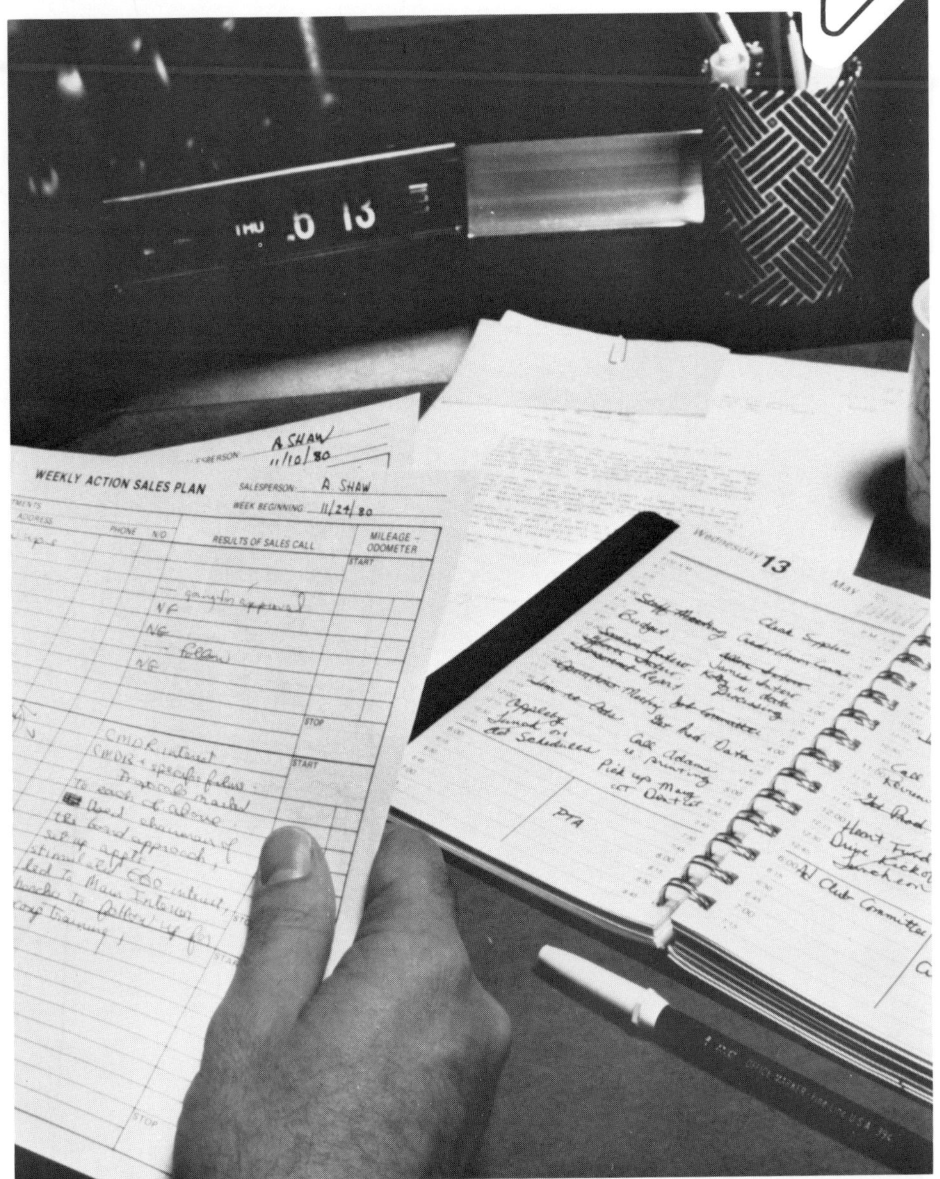

8 • Checking Results

Supervisors have three standard questions in starting a piece of work. What do we have to get done? How much time do we have? And what do we have to work with? Without these guidelines they know they would have no way to measure progress and check results. They recognize the irony of the saying: "If you don't know where you're going, any road will get you there." Supervisors and managers plan their moves ahead of time and then get the job under way.

PRODUCTION GOALS

People like to check the tally sheet when they know what the score stands for. Employees produce better if they understand work objectives and can see progress. Wise supervisors have long made it a practice to enlist support by explaining production goals. They then break the work down into units to provide checkpoints along the way. Short-term scheduling is a common procedure for this purpose. People have a strong drive for completion and find satisfaction in finishing well-defined sections of longer jobs.

Work Standards

In addition to knowing the main goals for the job, employees look for standards by which to measure their own work and behavior—norms against which to play the game. Rules of conduct, for example, reach new people by way of handbooks or word of mouth during their early days on the job, but what often are not spelled out are the standards for enforcement. Regulations may vary on things like starting times. Some supervisors expect their people to be directly at work stations when the hour comes; other accept arrival on the premises within a reasonable period. Standards are needed on other items also: safety procedures, wash-up time, phone calls, security, coffee breaks, and so forth. As a general practice, no rule can be considered in effect if clear notice of standards has not been given or if violations are tolerated.

Work Performance

Ideally, every supervisor should have a yardstick for measuring what workers accomplish. Otherwise, workers have no mark to meet and cannot be called to task for poor performance. This sounds simpler than it proves to be in practice.

On some straight production jobs, standards can be set for the number of units turned out. Sales and service people can also be checked by calls made, orders taken, or dollar volume. Rating forms are useful for this procedure when they list measurable items like attendance and quantity or quality of work. Rating forms cause trouble, however, when they ask for evaluations on such matters as judgment, attitude, or loyalty. Supervisors can only make guesstimates on these qualities, and the ratings are open to argument when discussed with workers. Employees not on production jobs have duties that are difficult to measure. Some statement is still in order, however, to define what constitutes satisfactory work on these assignments.

SATISFACTORY PERFORMANCE

For nonproduction jobs the best approach is to list the general conditions for acceptable performance. The first step in this process is to break the work down into its major parts. A secretary's duties, for example, might fall into the following classifications: (1) handling visitors and phone calls, (2) taking dictation, (3) typing, (4) filing, (5) record keeping, and (6) maintaining meeting and appointment schedules. Every job has a natural breakdown that can be worked out. Supervisors can find an outline of their own responsibilities by checking back to Chapter 1.

The second step is to list specific standards that will demonstrate satisfactory performance on each part of the job. For the secretary, standards for one aspect of the work might read as follows:

TYPING

Performance is satisfactory when the employee—

(1) Can demonstrate on request a speed of 60 wpm.
(2) Maintains an average of not more than one error per five pages of final typescript.
(3) Regularly checks for needed corrections in copy.
(4) Meets standard stenographic practice for spacing, centering, and style.
(5) Maintains typewriter in such condition that full and clear lettering results.

An important rule in listing standards is that they be made as specific as possible. General statements of performance should be avoided, as, for the secretary, that he or she does *a good typing job*. Adequate breakdowns can be worked out for almost every kind of work, and are useful to the supervisor in checking accomplishment.

STANDARDS SETTING

With facts in hand, supervisors can face rating interviews with less worry about arguments or challenges. Union stewards and employees themselves are more willing to accept necessary discipline and correction for the worker when the facts are there to support the action.

If the failure is one for which the group as a whole bears responsibility, the facts again are likely to influence the members and lead to changed behavior. A discussion of late starts, for example, along with better records in other groups, can lead to general improvement on tardiness. Groups respond to clear evidence of their shortcomings and try to improve—when the standard is known.

Factfinding

Most supervisors resist record keeping, but there is no other way to keep track of progress and problems on the job. Reports based on accurate and complete records are what the organization needs for planning and control. By putting together input from all parts of the operation, management can get the big picture and make the necessary moves.

s are the key in this procedure; they supply the ns are based. The same supervisors can use their oblems of their own. They can pinpoint time and ake corrections.

a continuing problem. It can dribble away when by (1) delays for equipment repairs or slow deliveries, quired by employee error, machine failure, or faulty material; and (3) production gaps caused by absenteeism and turnover. The records will show what caused the problem.

Poor workmanship and loafing also pose problems for the supervisor. Training, clearer standards, and stronger motivation are the probable answers in these cases. Other delays are procedural and call for improved layout or better systems for maintenance or communication.

All these difficulties show up in one form or another in nearly every kind of work. What is needed by the supervisor is an organized way to get the facts and find answers. This is problem solving.

Five-Step Pattern

There are several different systems being offered for solving job problems. In broad outline all of them follow the same logical pattern from sizing up the situation to selecting the best solution and starting corrective action. The five steps listed here will give supervisors a useful tool for tackling most of their difficulties.

(1) State the Trouble

Defined as too much overtime, frequent mix-ups, equipment failures, late starts, or whatever. This is evidence of a problem, not the problem itself.

(2) List the Facts

Study the records, talk with the people, call in experts, observe, and make notes.

(3) Define the Problem

Analyze the facts, discard nonessentials, narrow down to a best estimate of probable cause. Half the solution comes from determining the real problem.

(4) Pick the Best Solution

Go over possible ways to remove the cause of the trouble; select the one with the best chance of success. Consider side effects before a tryout.

(5) Put It to Work

Set up a plan of action for making the correction: how it will be carried out and results checked.

Doctors follow this same procedure day after day. The patient is ill, and the physician is faced with a problem-solving situation. All doctors start by making a diagnosis, which is another way of saying they look for the cause of the difficulty. They get the facts by asking questions, checking pulse and temperature, testing blood pressure, and so on. And finally, they use the facts to determine the trouble and complete their diagnoses. Only after finding the cause or real problem will a doctor start treatment.

Supervisors may become impatient at taking this much time. Actually, an organized approach saves time in the long run and has a better chance of success than guesswork. No one wants a doctor who jumps to conclusions on treatments, and no supervisor can be considered reliable who makes decisions without analyzing the situation. The only exception is when fast action is required during emergencies.

EMPLOYEE CONDUCT AND PERFORMANCE

Supervisors usually find it easier to deal with failures of equipment and procedure than they do with people problems. They can be logical about finding solutions to the former, but when workers are involved, their first instinct is to blame and punish the offenders. The purpose should be the same in both cases—to find the cause in order to correct the situation and to prevent the trouble from continuing.

Work groups expect regular checks to be made on conduct and performance. When there is a failure or violation, they also expect firm and fair correction. What they resent is so-called yo-yo enforcement, up one day and down the next. What bothers them even more is having no clear basis used in the first place for measuring behavior or results. Standards are fundamental to effective systems of work control and can best be established with the cooperation of the group itself.

Discipline

When there is clear evidence of failure or misconduct, the supervisor is required to take appropriate action. This is an unpleasant duty but one that has to be faced. Nothing is gained and much can be lost by avoiding the issue. The objective is to influence the employee to change, not to get rid of him or her. Turnover is costly, and an effort should be made to save an established worker.

There are four stages in the disciplinary procedure:

(1) Discussion

The supervisor sits down with the employee and talks over the problem. If the employee is weak or careless in doing the work, the supervisor coaches. If behavior on the job is unacceptable, the supervisor acts as counselor. If a reprimand is in order, the supervisor administers it.

(2) Warning

If no change occurs as a result of discussion, the supervisor notifies the employee of corrective action to follow if a change is not made. Accompanying this is an oral warning which gives the employee a limited time to improve. The warning is noted in the supervisor's records, and the employee is placed under observation. If again there is no change, a written warning is issued stating similar terms. This is official and is entered in the employee's record with copies provided to all parties concerned.

(3) Discipline

When the warning period runs out without favorable results, penalties are invoked. These may include suspension, demotion, transfer, loss of pay, or other action. The purpose of all warnings and penalties is to influence the employee to mend his or her ways. Some individuals require the full treatment before they try to reform.

(4) Dismissal

This is the final move, of course, and is simply the supervisor's last resort in correcting the situation. No action should be taken in the first place beyond Stage 1 (discussion and reprimand) unless the supervisor is prepared to go all the way to dismissal, if necessary. If the supervisor is willing to live with the trouble rather than lose the employee, warnings or discipline should not be started. Failure to follow through on warnings will mean complete loss of effectiveness with the group. The supervisor will be recognized for what he or she is—a paper tiger.

Handling Money

Unless cash transactions are part of daily duties, most first-line supervisors are not called on to check accounts. They do need to watch costs, but overall financial controls are usually left to the front office. Matters like sales revenues, operating ratios, and return on investment are not in the province of the supervisor.

Controls are required in retail operations, of course, when employees have access to the till. One supervisor of a chain of food stands pointed up his responsibility this way: "When I put a new operator at one of our locations, he soon gets an idea of taking over the place for himself. His tune on the cash register goes like this: 'First a nickel and then a dime, and by and by she'll all be mine.' It's my job to change his tune so the last line reads 'to help the business every time.' " The checking procedure generally involves a regular inventory of supplies measured against sales records. In the food chain mentioned, sandwich sales can be checked by the number of buns gone from stock, and pies and cakes can be precut as a control feature.

Pilferage

There is no easy way to handle fraud and theft problems. Supervisors may try to avoid being labeled "snoopervisors" in these matters and end up with a reputation as "easy marks." Alert attention to security matters is the best pattern to follow. This puts potential offenders on notice and tends to keep losses down.

Most employees are honest, but careless supervisors can put unfair temptations in their way. Open shelves and containers literally invite pilferage. Employees who are caught "borrowing" sometimes explain that they did not want what they were taking. It was just too readily available to resist.

There are several steps supervisors can take to keep things under control. Here are some common-sense procedures:

Check on any visitors or delivery people who hang around more than a reasonable time. They may be picking up items or accepting goods passed to them by employees.

Look into convenient hiding places from time to time. Fuse boxes and restroom cabinets are favorite spots for caching small objects.

Follow up on invoices received for goods or services. See that deliveries were made and work was performed as listed. Fraud by collusion is all too common a practice.

At irregular periods make spot checks of inventories on hand. Provide a routine system for employees to check out stock and equipment. If loans of tools are permitted for personal use, see that conditions are met for return or replacement.

Some employees may even feel that pilferage is justified from big operations. They will give various explanations and excuses if caught. Supervisors have a responsibility to state clearly that theft is theft and will be so considered when cases arise.

WORK PROCEDURES

Supervisors need to check on their people, but checks on procedure will also be necessary. Procedural errors can be disturbing to a supervisor because they offer evidence that his or her planning was faulty in the first place. The layout may not be leading to a smooth flow of work, supplies may not be feeding in on schedule, handling of materials may be awkward, inspection may be faulty, or the tie-in with other departments may not be working properly.

Improvements in work organization are the business of the supervisor. The maintenance of a strong progressive system requires alertness to problems, openness to suggestions, and willingness to change. Just how important this is will be developed in our next section.

Check List . . . checking results

1. Set goals for the job. What needs to be done?
2. Break the work down into units. Use short-term scheduling.
3. State rules of conduct at the location. Give standards for enforcement.
4. On production jobs, show workers the norms expected in quantity and quality.
5. For nonproduction jobs, break the work into its major parts.
6. Then list conditions or evidence of satisfactory performance on each part.
7. Keep full records of work progress and problems.
8. In solving problems, get the facts and identify causes before acting.
9. Use discussion to correct poor work or conduct. Start discipline only if prepared to go all the way.
10. Set procedures and maintain controls for handling money and supplies.

9 · MAKING IMPROVEMENTS

9 • Making Improvements

One measure of a manager is his or her ability to initiate change. No supervisor should be satisfied to finish a year without some improvements in the operation. There are two directions to move in uncovering areas to investigate. First, you can observe the work personally to find problems that need attention. Second, you can establish a climate for change, one in which your people feel free to come up with ideas. A group takes its cue on this from the leader. Do you want to keep things as they are, or are you really looking for a better way?

THE QUESTIONING APPROACH

In checking work, supervisors need to examine every step with such questions in mind as these: Why is this done? How is it done? Can it be omitted? What would make it better? They look for changes that will cut costs, save time, eliminate duplication, reduce waste, promote sales or public favor, improve quality, or make the operation safer.

Where to Look

Special attention can be given to the trouble spots. Bottlenecks are good places to start, areas where there are delays, downtime, low output. Tools and equipment, poor layout, or too much record keeping may be the problem. On this last, it is well recognized that oversystematizing can delay an otherwise smooth flow of work.

Leads on problems can come directly from the workers themselves. Complaints need to be listened to and checked out. Accidents and absences are worth analyzing. One point deserving emphasis is the value of looking at repetitive jobs where many items are moved through in a day. A small correction in this procedure can pile up large savings.

What to Look for

In sizing up the operation, supervisors may see some obvious weak spots. Long transportation processes usually need correction. Back-tracking is another evidence of faulty layout. Poor access to storage and an unsteady flow of supplies are others. Still others are wasted motions and awkward work positions by employees.

Charts and Diagrams

Flow studies are not useful where work is done almost entirely at one station. In many office jobs, however, and in most field and plant work, there is a chain of operations that can be studied. Charts or diagrams can be prepared in these cases to help in pointing out trouble spots. For example, the process depicted in Figure 4 is a common one in most offices—filling out a form for the bosses' signature. A trouble spot here might be the delay encountered as form X sits in one in/out box after another while waiting for messenger pickup.

Flow charting is a process of listing the steps in an operation and marking down the time involved and distance traveled. A simple chart can be worked out for this purpose. (see Figure 4) Five standard symbols are employed to mark each step. These are ○ for operation, → for transportation, □ for inspection, D for delay, and ▽ for storage. An operation usually involves (1) make ready, (2) job tasks, and (3) cleanup. All of these should be included on the chart.

The steps are listed on the charts along with time, distance, and the symbol for each. This is followed by careful study of each part and of the process as a whole to determine where changes can be made. A challenging attitude should be brought to the study with possible changes noted as the analysis continues. After this, a revised chart can be prepared listing the steps, time, and distances as they appear with all changes applied. Differences in time and travel can then be marked to show how much would be gained under the new system.

A flow diagram is just what the name implies, a picture of the operation with lines following the path of the job unit as it travels through the different steps. The standard symbols can be used along each path with numbers on the "do" part of the operation. Scale drawings are best, but the picture need not be a finished draftsman's product. The value of diagramming is that long stretches of travel and

Figure 4. **Simplified Flow Process Chart**

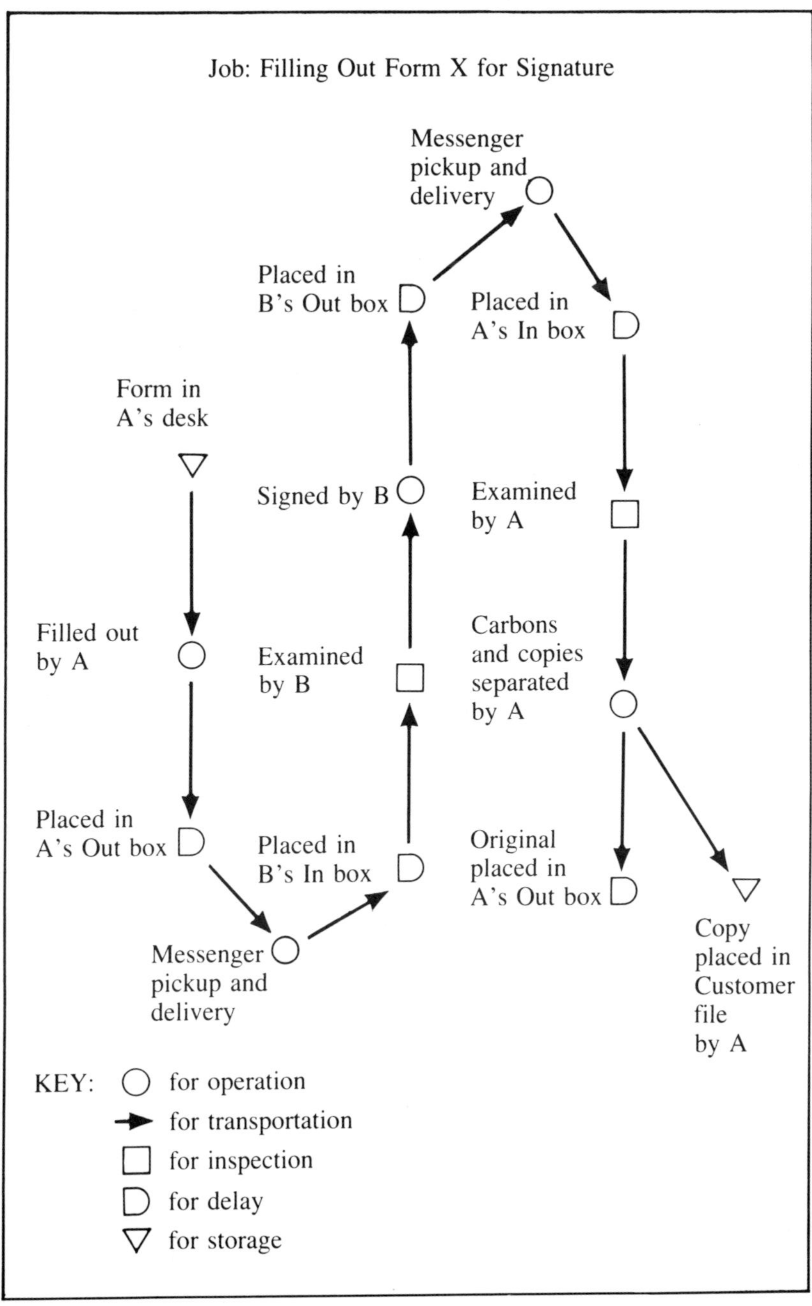

backtracking show up plainly. The layout can be more easily seen for planning changes in location of work stations and equipment Some supervisors have also found scale models useful for trying out moves ahead of time.

FACT AND FANCY

There are probably a dozen techniques like these for sizing up work situations. Motion economy studies, multiple activity charts, work distribution charts, work sampling, and others are all useful ways of gathering facts. Facts alone, however, are not enough. There has to be a recombining of these elements into something different before an improvement plan can take shape. This calls for a creative mind.

Putting Imagination to Work

Creativity, for one thing, is the ability to find new content in old packages. Given a situation to improve, creative individuals bring to bear everything they have ever heard, seen, or experienced and ask themselves the question: How could this be made different? Their imaginations work on the problem and come up with a variety of possible changes. The first purpose will be to spark as many new ideas as possible; criticizing them and judging their value will come later.

Creativity requires concentration. Some supervisors have the ability to focus on a problem and to blot out all the noise and confusion around them. For most, the ideas come better when they are away from the job and can turn the situation over in their minds and look at it from all angles. This has the added advantage of breaking contact with present practice. The main block to planning out new methods for handling the work is the persistence of old methods to get in the way. Established systems die hard.

The Critical Stage

Only after the mind has brought forth a number of new approaches to the problem should judgment be called into play. This is the critical stage when the ideas are examined, analyzed, and mentally tried out on the job. Costs are listed and results with possible side effects are considered. The idea selected for tryout is the one with the best chance of success. Measures of the total result against present practice will show what gains will result. The next problem is a key one—how to get support for the new procedure from management and the workers.

The SOS Factors

Management judges change by its effect on the business. If dollar improvements can be shown and the new plan presented clearly, approval is almost certain. Management studies the SOS (sales or savings) factors in every proposal. In other words, what management wants is lower costs or higher output. Any move that shows improvements in these elements will be looked on with favor.

The mistake most supervisors make is in offering new procedures without detailing the financial advantages. Management is naturally negative toward propositions that have to be accepted on faith. Even nonprofit operations, where competition and gain are not important, still find that management welcomes improvements in costs and productivity.

Resistance to Change

Workers have different concerns from management about altering the job. What they want to know is how the new move will affect them as individuals. People do not resist change; they resist being changed. Their reasons are natural and apply to any of us in our work.

In the first place, habits are hard to break, whether at work or any place else. We tend to cling to familiar patterns. We are afraid we will not understand the new system nor be able to perform under it successfully. The questions we ask are these: "What's wrong with the old way?" "How can you prove this new system is any better?" There are even feelings that the proposed procedure is a personal criticism of us and the job we have been doing.

Most of all, we resist change when it comes unexpectedly and we have not been involved in planning it. We vote down good ideas or help them to fail because the way was not prepared for us to accept and support the new system. Improvement-minded supervisors can save themselves headaches by following these simple rules for introducing change.

Wherever possible, get the group involved in working out the procedure. Talk over the problem and draw out ideas. Everybody likes to get into the act and may have suggestions to offer.

Make certain the change is understood. Explain the reasons for it and the way it will affect everybody on the job.

Make the move slowly. Give plenty of advance notice and time for people to get used to the idea.

Start with a tryout. Most people want to be fair and give a new idea a chance to prove its worth.

Report results fairly and completely. If they are favorable, announce details of the permanent changeover.

Selling a change is as important as creating the system in the first place. Many a workable idea has gone down the drain for want of acceptance. The wise supervisor plans ahead and moves carefully in introducing improvements.

THE SUGGESTION SYSTEM

Management and supervision have no monopoly on brains in the establishment. A sound suggestion system can go far toward bringing out the best thinking of the whole team. Whether an award plan is followed or public recognition is given for usable ideas, a procedure for processing employee proposals can be a boon to an organization. Prerequisites are a welcoming attitude toward new thinking and confidence on the part of workers that management will handle their ideas in a fair and equitable manner.

Supervisors who resent new proposals as reflections on their own ability, or who grab the credit when a good idea is put forward, will get little business in the suggestion department. Improvement-minded groups do not grow that way by chance. It takes planning and effort to develop a favorable climate for change.

INERTIA VS. IMPROVEMENT

''Don't rock the boat'' is a common expression in many organizations. People in a slow-moving operation like to drift peacefully on a sea of inertia. Killer phrases are used to block any efforts toward change. Here are a few of the common ones:

It won't work!
We've tried it before!
It's too far ahead!
It's too old-fashioned!
What's the matter with the way it is now?
We've never done it that way!
Let's sleep on it!

The last is exactly what the outfit will do if management is not willing to push in new directions. The supervisor should be the natural action leader in the group in these cases, and will be if he or she recognizes that planned progress is another name for effective management.

UNION PARTICIPATION

Unions do not resist change when they are informed and can see benefits for their members. Improvement in safety or any chance for members to share in the gains will bring support from the wiser union leaders. Reduction in the number of jobs is always troublesome, but even objections to this can be overcome when longer-term advantages for the rank and file can be shown. There will always be some shortsighted union representatives to deal with, and this is part of the problem considered in our next section.

Check List... making improvements

1. Try to make some improvements every year.

2. Study trouble spots—bottlenecks, rework, hazards, downtime.

3. Look for long transportation, backtracking, wasted motions.

4. Use charts and diagrams to analyze work flow.

5. Block out old methods. Think of different approaches.

6. Test new ideas mentally on the job. List costs, results, and side effects.

7. Show management the values in lower costs, better output, higher sales.

8. Give workers a part in planning a change. Talk it through.

9. Try out a new system first. Install it only if it works.

10. Push for change. Supervisors are the action leaders.

10 · DEALING WITH UNIONS

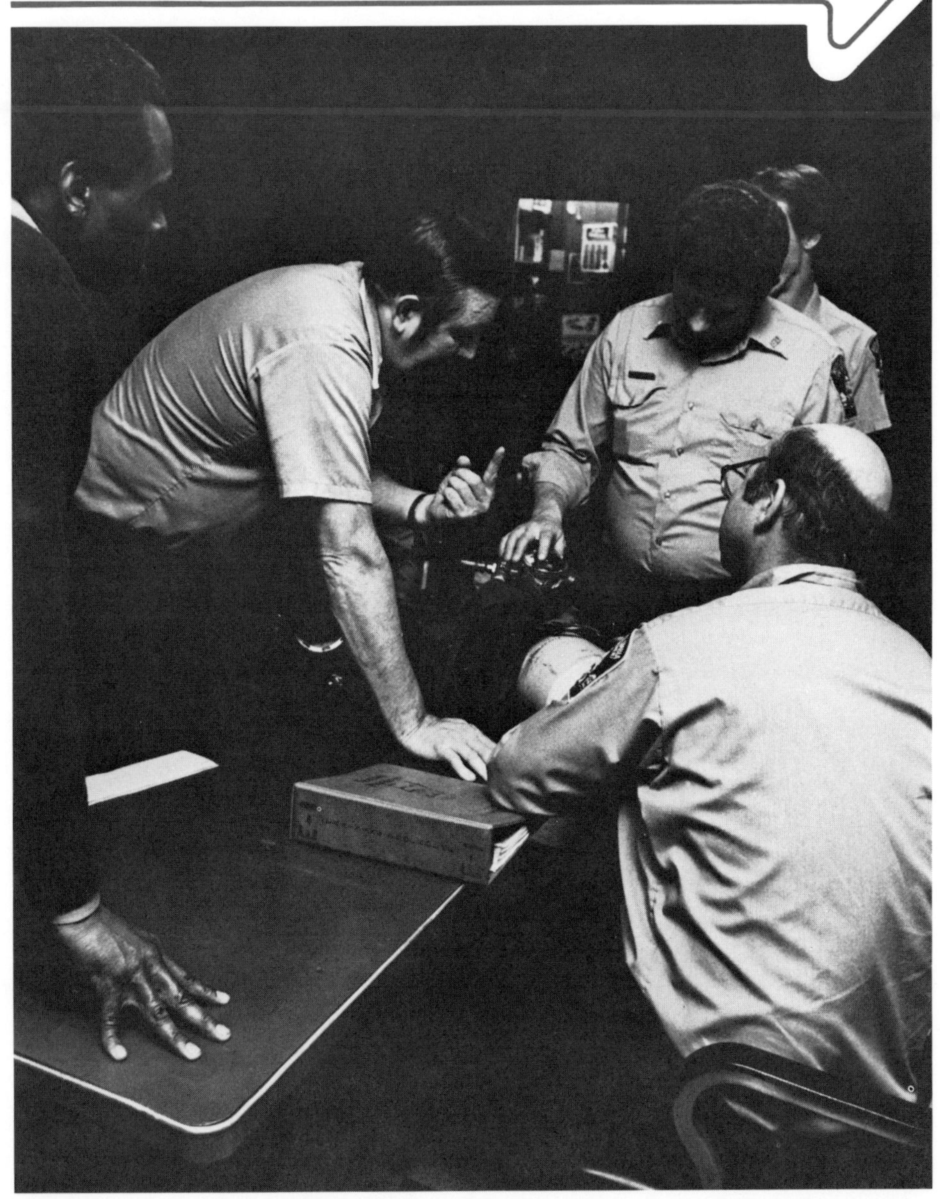

10 • Dealing With Unions

Unions are here to stay, and supervisors will need to reckon with them. They are part of the management job. Of the nation's work force, 24.2 million are now covered by approximately 193 thousand union-management contracts spread across the country. This takes in about 22 percent of all employees. Small businesses have been less affected, and white-collar workers are only partly organized, but the broad influence of unionism is still considerable.

Supervisors have a continuing relationship with the issue of unionization. They have a part to play before, during, and after unionization takes place. Before it happens, they are called on to manage their operations in such a way that employees will see no value in forming a local. If organizing does get under way, they are expected to counter the move but still avoid any charges of unfair labor practice. And finally, if their groups go ahead and vote in the union, they have the job of working effectively under the contract with the officers, stewards, and committee members of the local.

WHY WORKERS JOIN UNIONS

The main reason union members now give is to secure protection from arbitrary action by management. In other words, to keep from being pushed around. In earlier times the purpose was "to get a living wage," but this is seldom a cause for action any more. There are still problems, but the basic needs of employed people are pretty well covered today in our affluent society.

There are a variety of other influences that lead individuals to join unions. Some want to feel they have a say about conditions of employment. Others join because of group pressures and the desire to be a part of the lodge. A few are looking for status by winning election to union office. In closed- or agency-shop situations, of course, employees have no choice but to sign up. And public employees may have straight economic objectives where taxpayers have been unreasonably slow in funding wage increases.

WHAT UNIONS CAN CONTRIBUTE

There are good and bad unions, as in every other organized activity. A strong local can be a positive influence and benefit for all parties concerned. It can promote the business as well as protect the rights of workers. It can serve as a watchdog on management and also strengthen the enterprise in which its members hold their jobs. Fortunately, there are sound and constructive union bodies in existence; if this were not so, the whole movement would lose ground.

A weak union, on the other hand, tries to upgrade itself by tearing down the parent organization. It builds a hostility barrier between its members and management and leads employees away from support for the business of which they are a part. Usually this is caused by plain short-sightedness on the part of officers and business agents, although political abuses and force within the union can play a part where the membership is not on guard.

Whatever the climate of the local, you as the supervisor are charged with maintaining good relations. You, as well as the union, represent employees and look after their interests. Your objective is still the production of goods or services along with job satisfaction for the people working under you. To carry this out effectively is a difficult and challenging task.

THE ONE IN THE MIDDLE

Supervisors are a part of management. There can be no question about this despite the natural desire to be part of the group. Your job is different now, and you carry the badge of authority. If you are competent at the work, however, and strong enough to admit when you are wrong, you have a good start toward succeeding in your new relationship with employees—unionized or otherwise.

Long-range goals of management and the union should be similar: steady work and fair pay for employees under favorable operating conditions and with reasonable satisfaction for investors and customers. The problems come when workers and management fail to see eye to eye on priorities for meeting these requirements. Supervisors may recognize merit in union demands and still understand that the overall needs of the business call for something different.

The Strike Emergency

Problems are especially troublesome during a strike, when feelings run high. Supervisors who have been promoted out of union ranks find the tugs and pulls of old loyalties hard to set aside. They are also faced with the necessity for maintaining good relations with strikers, who will be back working under them as soon as the difficulty is past. Steady attention to business is the best pattern to follow during these periods.

No words or acts should be offered that could aggravate the situation. At the same time, appropriate action must be taken whenever strike behavior goes beyond legal limits. In most situations a sound approach for the supervisor is to continue on an open and friendly basis, carry out the job as required, and welcome the crew back when the trouble is over.

The Collective Bargaining Agreement

Supervisors have rights and duties in the day-to-day application of the contract. Your first responsibility, of course, is to know the terms of the collective bargaining agreement. This includes review of all changes when a new contract is negotiated. The basis on which you operate is that management has the right to make all decisions in carrying on the work, and the union has the right to protest any decision that it considers to be in violation of the terms. Disagreements are to be worked out between steward and supervisor whenever possible. If there is still a difference of opinion, the grievance machinery provides a way to clear up the question.

An alert supervisor will exercise the rights of management. Failure to do so will result in establishment of an unfavorable practice. Supervisors can negate a contract by allowing abuses to continue. Workers normally cannot refuse to obey an order and stewards cannot countermand one unless compliance is against the law or could result in bodily harm. On any change in work practice, the supervisor should check the agreement to see if it is permitted. If there is doubt, advice should be sought.

Relations with most stewards can be kept on a friendly and businesslike footing. Some union representatives are trained in the care and feeding of foremen, but supervisors who maintain their position and go about their jobs in a straightforward fashion need have little concern about losing out in an exchange. Stewards should be kept informed of all new developments, but their approval should not be requested. There are joint-determination clauses in some contracts, but normally the supervisor runs the operation completely. Occasionally a steward or committee member may be out to make a name by stirring up grievances. As long as they operate within the contract, supervisors do best to ride with the action, no matter how many petty complaints they encounter.

Documentation

It is important to maintain a complete record system. Notes should be made with date of entry on every personnel action: change of assignment, disciplinary move, introduction of new methods or equipment, and others. A good practice is to keep a daily log with transfer of items as needed to individual files. The folder for each worker should include his or her production record, attendance, wage changes, discipline, health, and other items.

Records are of first importance in grievance proceedings and at formal hearings before arbitrators. What are looked for in both cases are the facts as related to the intent of the contract. With notes in good order, the supervisor can establish the case and leave contract interpretations to the authorities. The supervisor's written reply to a grievance should include a brief statement of the situation, reasons for the decision, and a summary.

In operating under a union contract, supervisors may find smooth sailing and few problems. On the other hand, they may wish the day had never come when they were burdened with so many problems and grievances in getting the work done. There is no question that managing in a unionized situation can be more costly and time-consuming than straight operation—some say as high as 20 percent more. A question to consider is how it might have been avoided in the first place.

HOW TO MAKE UNIONIZING UNNECESSARY

In simple terms this means running the job in such a way that workers do not feel pushed around. Except for traditional union situations in the craft and industrial fields, employees are not eager to pay dues and give up the right to independent action. They move in the union's direction only when they feel management is taking advantage and not listening.

Evidence indicates little progress in the spread of unionization over the past 20 years. An exception may be found in public-service occupations, where gains for workers in the past had been slower. For the rest, management has moved in two directions. Where the unions are already entrenched and demands have become unreasonable, managers have been forced to reduce manpower by the use of new methods and equipment. A second approach has been to emphasize fuller information for employees and more involvement in planning the work.

The main push toward unionizing comes when employees are subject to favoritism and arbitrary handling by supervisors. Management decisions are made by whim and caprice, and there is a general climate of mistrust. These are conditions that lead workers to call in the organizers and sign interest cards. Most group leaders know better today and go out of their way to operate with their people on a team basis. Problems and plans are worked out together. Overtime is evenly distributed. Pay and progression are fairly administered, and communications are open and complete. The supervisor comes on the job to help and to listen to suggestions and complaints. If this sounds like an ideal situation, it is, but well within reach of today's group leaders. Even with an unfavorable management climate, people respond to fair treatment and straight talk from their own supervisors. As a matter of fact, organizers avoid coming into places where employee relations are healthy.

DO'S AND DON'TS DURING THE ORGANIZING PERIOD

Once organizers make contact or employees begin forming their own bargaining unit, supervisors are constrained by labor laws and decisions from engaging in certain conduct to stop the movement. They may still state the arguments against unionizing but may not try to influence the vote by pressure or promises.

Here is what supervisors can do:

Tell employees that they prefer to deal with them directly on a personal basis rather than through some outside agency.

Tell employees how their wages, benefits, and working conditions compare with others.

Tell employees of disadvantages that may result from joining a union: strikes, picketing, dues, fines, and assessments.

Tell employees that no union can guarantee employment or set pay for a given job.

Correct any untrue or misleading statement or propaganda that has been issued.

Distribute reprints of articles or reports about unions.

Tell employees they are free to join or not to join, that signing a union authorization card or application does not bind them to vote for the union in an election.

Outline the NLRB election procedures and emphasize the importance of voting.

Make or enforce rules regarding solicitation of membership during work hours.

Enforce rules, lay off, and discharge, so long as customary practice in these matters is followed.

Hold meetings of the group to discuss the union question except during the 24 hours preceding the election.

Restrict union organizers from contacting employees on company premises not open to the public and during working hours.

Here is what supervisors cannot do:

Promise employees pay increases, promotions, or favors for voting against the union.

Suggest any loss of benefits or privileges or threaten employees for supporting the union.

Discriminate by imposing undesirable transfers or assignments upon employees showing interest in the union.

Show partiality in any way to employees not interested in the union over those who are.

Attempt to separate by transfer or assignment employees favoring the union from those not committed.

Ask employees what they think about a union or its officers.

Ask employees how they intend to vote or what they know about other employees' thoughts or intentions.

Ask employees at the time of hiring or later whether they belong to a union or have signed applications or authorization cards.

Ask employees about meetings or affairs of the union.

Urge employees to persuade others to oppose the union.

Prevent employees from soliciting union memberships on the premises when they are on their own time and there is no interference with the work.

Bar union representatives from talking with employees on their free time in any part of the premises open to the public.

THE MANAGEMENT-UNION CLIMATE

In all these situations—before, during, and after organizing has taken place—you will be called on to follow the prevailing attitudes of your management toward dealing with unions. Some companies take a position of fighting unions and trying to break them. Others tolerate or accommodate to the relationship but are careful to protect their rights both in negotiating and administering a contract. A few have moved to a cooperative arrangement under which they work with unions to make the enterprise successful. Most companies today have taken the middle road and accept the union as part of the conditions for doing business.

Both new companies and established ones are working hard to stem the spread of unionism. This is healthy for the employees, since they receive favorable treatment without the necessity for organizing. The quality of supervision in these situations plays a strong part in convincing workers that a union would offer no advantage.

A TEST FOR SUPERVISORS

Whether working with unions or making them unnecessary, supervisors face both a challenge and an opportunity in the area of labor relations. They operate on the front line of management and are in a position to set favorable conditions for productivity and job satisfaction. Effective supervisors look after their people with or without a union to keep check.

Check List... dealing with unions

1. As a supervisor you are part of management. Represent the organization to your group.

2. Before and during organizing, try to operate so employees will see no need for unionizing.

3. If a local is still formed, work as well as possible under the contract.

4. Begin by studying terms of agreement and determining application.

5. Run the operation and make all work decisions.

6. On actions considered to violate the contract, recognize the union's right to grieve.

7. Keep management's rights in effect and correct work abuses as they occur.

8. Maintain full records for use in grievance and arbitration hearings.

9. During strikes, pay steady attention to business and give no undue aggravation to those off the job.

10. Regularly look after the interests of your people with or without a union to keep check.

11 · HANDLING PROBLEM EMPLOYEES

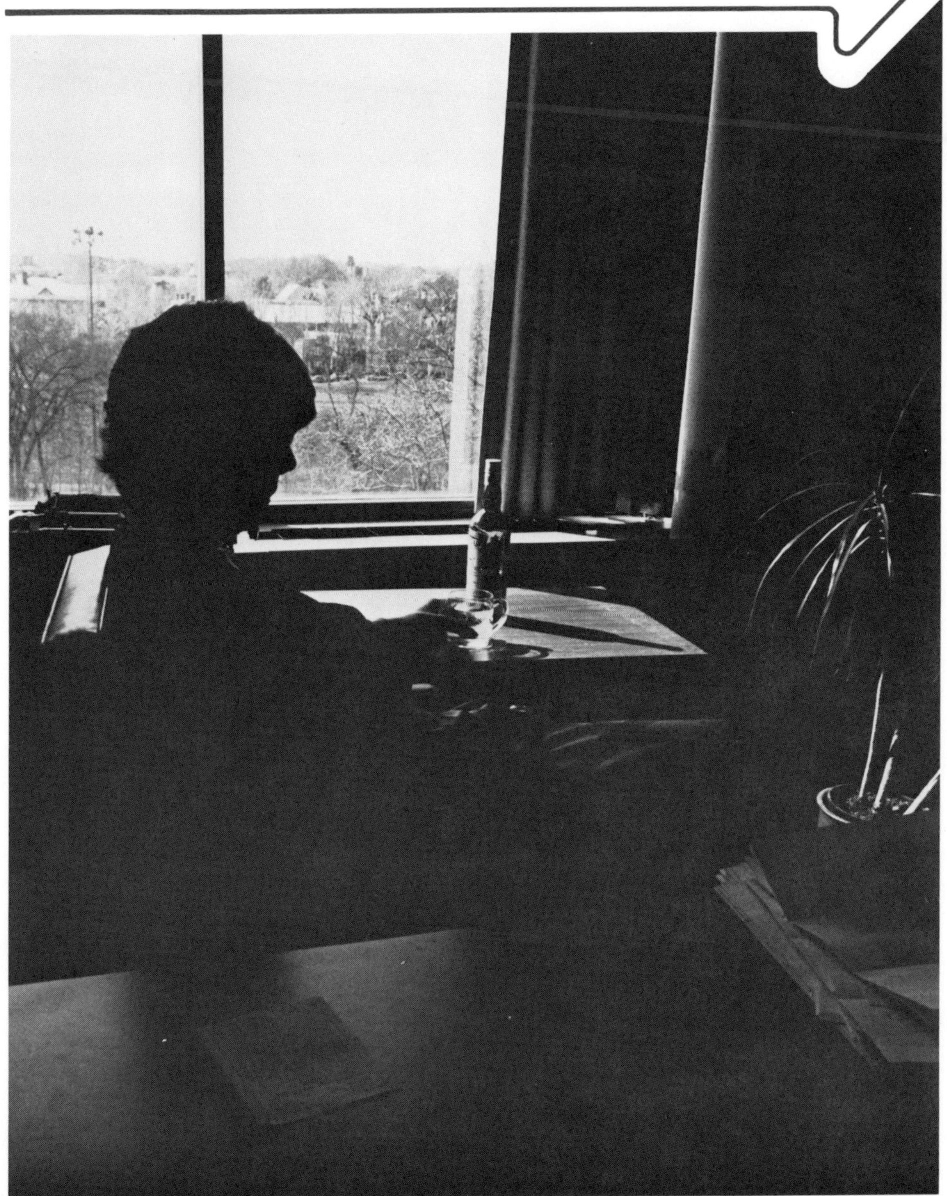

11 • Handling Problem Employees

Employees bring their own pressures and problems with them to the job. These cover the full range of troublesome attitudes, habits, and weaknesses that plague the human race. Most workers keep these matters under control and avoid letting them affect the work. When abnormal or excessive behavior does come out, however, supervisors are forced to step in and take action. Fortunately only a few employees become real problem cases, normally five percent or less.

CAUSES FOR ACTION

The standard procedure is for supervisors to stay out of personal concerns unless there is real disturbance to the work. Causes for action are unsafe practices, low performance, property loss, chronic absenteeism, and behavior that has a negative effect on the work group or the public.

Most organizations have disciplinary procedures to cover flagrant offenses such as theft, assault, organized gambling, and sale of drugs or alcohol. When proof is clear, violators are dismissed without question. The difficult problems for the supervisor come from the range of situations that are not open and shut: borrowing of tools from the job, use of pep pills and depressants, drinking at lunch, and other borderline actions.

Some of the common situations and problems are outlined below. In all cases where proof is not clear or correction is still possible, supervisors should avoid hasty action. The best approach is to start building a case with notes and dates on related happenings. When the evidence becomes significant, it should be reviewed with higher management.

If proof is complete and a serious violation of law or policy has occurred, dismissal is in order. If the offense is minor or there is a chance for change of behavior, the procedure to follow is standard. First a straight talk with the employee ending with a question on how matters can be put right. If a referral is needed, as in the case of alcoholism, arrangements are made. In a serious situation an oral warning is given. If the behavior continues, a written warning follows with a copy to the employee and, if the group is organized, a copy to the union. Any further offense is cause for disciplinary action.

One piece of advice to supervisors deserves emphasis. If there is no real intention of going as far as discipline or dismissal, only an interview should be held. Otherwise later threats of action have little effect. The offender loses respect for authority the same as the child who is warned of penalties which never come.

THE PROBLEM DRINKER

Once the compulsion to drink excessively becomes established and there is dependence on liquor, the victim of the habit is considered an alcoholic and the condition a disease. True alcoholics can seldom become controlled drinkers. Their only safety lies in complete abstinence. The problems they bring to the work place are well known, the most troublesome being long and unexpected absences. Alcoholics are often good workers and well liked until the disease begins to take over.

What are the signs of progressive alcoholism? First comes repeated drunkenness; the individual seldom stops at a moderate intake of alcohol. This is followed by drinking in the morning and sneaking drinks. Blackouts occur after which the drinker cannot remember where he or she was and what was said or done. Finally come the binges and benders with absences of a few days to weeks at a time. This is the time when guidance is needed, despite the drinker's opinion to the contrary. Unless help is made available, the slide down from this point is steep and fast.

When the facts are clear, supervisors can best serve by taking three steps:

Review the case with higher management.

If authorized to go ahead, get names and addresses of AA chapters or alcoholic treatment clinics in the area.

Have a straight talk with the individual in private and lay the facts on the table. State that if help is sought from AA or other counselors, the employee will be allowed one more violation. If the employee does not get help, his or her next slip will be cause for dismissal.

This seems a harsh procedure, but it forces the individual to face reality. It is the kindest approach in the long run and can save the problem drinker and his or her family from untold misery and suffering.

DRUG USE

This is a difficult problem for the supervisor, since pep pills and tranquilizers are easily available and used by many people today. Doctors may prescribe drugs for a variety of human needs. There is evidence, however, that abuse is on the increase at work locations as well as outside. Supervisors should know a few simple facts on the subject as well as the actions required when use or sale is detected. While there is no clear agreement among medical authorities on drug effects, a few general statements can be offered.

There are three main types of drugs:

(1) The Stimulants

These include speed and pep pills as well as tea, coffee, and colas. The most dangerous one in this classification is cocaine. Users of stimulants develop more of a psychological craving than a physical need for the drug.

(2) The Depressants

These include the barbiturates and the opiates. Opiates are derived from the opium poppy or synthetics and include codeine, morphine, and heroin. The last has no medical use, and addiction is seldom cured. Users of opiates are understood to develop a real physical need for the drug.

(3) The Hallucinogens

These are mind-benders and have no proved medical use. Marijuana is a mild form; hashish is more potent. The acids, such as LSD and mescaline, are the insidious ones and can lead to panic, fears, and suicidal urges. Effects of these drugs may return weeks or months after taking. Physical dependence is not supposed to develop from the use of hallucinogens, but psychological needs are created.

The risk in discussing symptoms is that supervisors may begin suddenly to see drug users on all sides. As long as good judgment is applied, however, and a few cautions observed, rash action is not likely to be taken.

In the first place, a supervisor is always responsible for removing from the job any employee whose behavior he or she considers unsafe or disturbing. This action can be taken without question in suspected drug cases as well as in other cases. In the second place, an employee should never be accused of taking drugs. Instead, you should state that in your opinion the employee is unable to work effectively, may be ill, and must be relieved of his or her duties until cleared by proper medical authorities. Sale of drugs is a different problem and should be handled where proved as a legal or disciplinary matter.

There are a variety of signs and symptoms of drug abuse, none of which should be judged hastily. These include frequent absences, self-neglect, erratic behavior, and lowered work performance. Physical appearance may show dilated or constricted pupils, drowsiness, slurred speech, and nervousness. Dress and behavior may also give clues. Sunglasses and long sleeves worn at all times and frequent trips to the washroom are possible tipoffs. Marijuana smoke can be identified by its sweet pungent odor similar to that of burning rope. Unlike other drugs, the use of marijuana cannot be detected by urinalysis.

Possession of drugs by itself is not an offense. They must have been obtained illegally and be other than the popular items sold in drug stores. While supervisors should give what help they can to drug abusers, their main concern must be the correction of any condition affecting the work or disturbing the group. Proper action is removal of the questionable individual from the job and his or her referral for medical review.

MALINGERING

We have discussed the absence problem in general, but a special case in this category is the malingerer. This is the employee who pretends to be ill or injured in order to get extra money or avoid work. Supervisors need to be watchful for these smart operators, who often put on a convincing show.

When malingering is suspected, the supervisor's main recourse is to report the facts up the line for handling by management and medical people. Checking with the employee's own physician can best be done by another doctor. A careful study should be made of the previous employment record to find whether similar behavior has been practiced elsewhere.

Legal claims for special compensation may be put forward by the malingering employee. These are necessarily handled by lawyers and medical experts. The supervisor's part is to report the facts, no more and no less.

Malingering goes beyond chronic absenteeism by adding fraud and trickery to the list of causes. Regular absentees may be troubled by recurring physical troubles: colds, migraine headaches, menstrual problems, diabetes, or indigestion. Absentees are even more likely to be staying away because they do not like the work. The malingerer, on the other hand, is more calculating, setting out from the start to take advantage of the system and if possible to profit from its weaknesses.

Whatever may be the legal and medical implications, the supervisor's one clear defense against malingering is the work itself. If absence is sufficiently frequent, the supervisor has a reasonable basis for judging the employee to be unable to fill the job. Dismissal for nonattendance is a proper solution.

TROUBLEMAKING AND INSUBORDINATION

There are a variety of disturbing behaviors in this category. Probably the most serious are the anti-management attitudes such as undermining authority, flouting rules, and challenging orders—everything up to open insubordination. The insubordination cases are simple to handle; when there is no physical risk to the employee, defiance of a direct command calls for dismissal. Care should be taken, however, to make certain that the order was reasonable and clearly explained and that the offender is defying and not just questioning it. The problem in all these situations is one of degree. How far can the supervisor let the behavior go before calling time?

The answer comes in two parts. First, rule-happy supervisors invite trouble. When they impose regulations on everything from toilet time to conversation, they can expect challenges. These may simply be a sign that employees have spirit and want to be treated as adults. Second, if the working climate and morale are generally good, a boss-baiter is better checked early and without delay. A straight-out, private discussion may clear the air and place the individual on notice. If the trouble continues and the individual's work record is good, the supervisor is forced to base any action on the severity of the offense and need for the worker on the job. You should, however, study your own words and manner to be certain that you are not inviting insolent reactions. Once you decide to give an official warning, you should be prepared to continue, if necessary, all the way to final discharge.

Other troublemakers are fanatics, social reformers, and those suffering from nameless dreads and fears. Again, straight talk may be the answer, but referral is also a sound recommendation. In most cases the motivation for these behaviors is deep-seated and not likely to change simply because the individual has come to the work place.

Immature and retarded people may have problems with instructions and regulations, but they are not troublemakers in the real sense. Theirs is a failure of understanding, not of intent, and the supervisor has the responsibility to show concern and patience in fitting them to the work.

DRESS AND APPEARANCE

Every new generation brings some change in dress and appearance to the job. The younger group now entering the world of work is no different except possibly in the extremes to which they may go. Colorful clothes, sandals, long hair, jewelry, and other costuming have raised some problems for supervisors.

In general, this is an area where considerable tolerance should be practiced. Supervisors can properly set limitations that are viewed as reasonable by most employees. Safety and health protection might justify the exclusion of long hair and loose or scanty attire. Shoes may be required to avoid foot injury in heavy work. Reasonable standards may also be set where employees are in contact with the public and loss of business could result. Normal propriety may be a further ground for excluding some styles and forms of dress for office work.

As long as supervisors stay generally in tune with the times and offer sensible reasons for decisions, there should be little difficulty with rules on dress and appearance.

PERSONAL PROBLEMS

These can come from a hundred sources and may require the intervention of the supervisor if they affect the work. If the employee maintains his or her usual production and safety standards, however, and cooperates with others, the supervisor does best to stay out of personal affairs. Of course, if an employee comes to you with a problem, you should listen willingly and offer what assistance you can.

The variety of problems is endless, as any experienced supervisor can testify. Some are financial troubles, marital squabbles, difficulties with children, health worries, housing problems, care of parents, settling of estates, accident claims, and so on and on. In many cases, there may be some negative effect on the work. An employee whose mind is on other matters is more likely than others to make errors in judgment, engage in unsafe practices, or slack off on duties.

Whether you are invited to help or are forced to step in, your guiding rule should be not to tell such employees what to do but to help them find their own answers. You should listen well, ask questions, get the facts, and summarize the problem as you see it. You can point out consequences of possible actions and suggest services the employee may not know about. You should not take over the problem yourself, but you do have an interest in seeing it cleared up.

THE YOUNG WORKER

Some supervisors worry about their ability to handle young workers today. They see them as wild, irresponsible, and demanding of special privileges. Actually, young people are carrying to the work place the same problems of growth and adjustment as in the past. The only difference is a greater willingness to bring their doubts into the open and "tell it like it is." Adults with wise heads and sound hearts are still needed to guide them into responsible adulthood. There is no more important responsibility for the supervisor to meet. To do so, the first need is to understand the nature of young workers.

Physical development is still a problem for the late teens and young adults. They are in a period of rapid growth. Muscles and bones are growing and may not operate in harmony. Young people have size but not strength and may tire easily. Movements can be awkward and uncoordinated.

Emotional growth is also characterized by pulls in different directions. The main drive is to reach adulthood with all its rights and privileges, but its responsibilities are not yet understood. The individual is alternately unsure and aggressive, critical of self but reaching for independence. This is a time of seeking for values, daydreaming, and idealism. Again, the wise supervisor can do much to set examples and direct energies.

Mental growth and learning are at a peak. There will be differences in basic intelligence, but the young individual is at his or her best at grasping new skills and knowledge in this period. The supervisor can point to opportunities and help plan development. Good supervisors are usually effective in developing people, and young employees can be challenges to their best efforts. These guidelines can help in the process:

Never talk down to young people; deal with them in adult fashion.

Treat all problems and questions with honesty. Tell it like it is.

Take a personal interest in young people; want them to succeed to the best of their abilities.

Give all problems serious consideration; the mountains that the supervisor found long ago were only molehills may still loom large to young people finding their way.

THE OLD HAND

A developing practice is to keep older workers on the job as long as performance is adequate and they want to stay. This has to be done within the organization's policy limits, but companies are beginning to question the need for a set retirement age. Long-term employees are found to be better bets for production than inexperienced younger ones.

Some of the plus values for the older group are loyalty to the organization, lower turnover, and fewer errors in the work. Quantity may be down, but production is of a higher quality. It is true that absences tend to be longer, but frequency is less, with a resultant overall average below that of younger workers. Experienced people have been conditioned to work, and most of them welcome it as a way to fill empty time. Studies show that purposeful activity of this kind extends life expectancy and adds to self-respect for senior citizens.

Some negative factors do exist, but these are more than offset by the plus values already mentioned. One characteristic of older workers is a tendency to resist change. They are slower to adapt to new procedures but will adjust if given information ahead of time. Training time is also longer, and there is some loss of speed and agility in both mental and physical effort.

Supervisors can do much to make this a fruitful period for both the worker and the organization. The values are obvious. Experienced people will serve as a steadying influence on the group and can assist in training and in planning the work. If necessary, transfers can be made to lighter duties with suitable adjustments in pay. When aging finally takes over and the work becomes too heavy, termination is in order. The supervisor is the best judge and can arrange the exit tactfully if he or she has maintained healthy contact with the individual.

People and problems are the chief components of the supervisors' job. If you had neither to deal with, you would be out of business. When people are the problems, you have an extra duty to help them straighten out for their own and their families' benefit. Your main responsibility is to the work itself and to the 95 percent of the employees who perform well on the job. Helping workers in trouble, however, will remain one of the chief satisfactions to be derived from your work.

Check List... handling problem employees

1. Step in when employee behavior causes real disturbance to the work.

2. Dismiss workers who commit proved illegal acts.

3. Allow alcoholics an extra slip if they join AA or accept treatment.

4. Refer suspected drug users for medical review if their work is off. Avoid open accusations of drug taking.

5. Terminate malingerers who have excessive absence. Keep facts for legal reference.

6. If work conditions are healthy, deal with minor troublemakers by private discussion.

7. Help people with personal problems to work out *their own* answers.

8. Take no action if you are not prepared to go as far as discipline or dismissal.

9. Give younger and older workers extra time. They can make good contributions.

10. Problem people and people with problems are part of the supervisor's job. Handling them correctly can bring real satisfaction.

12 · SUPPORTING THE ORGANIZATION

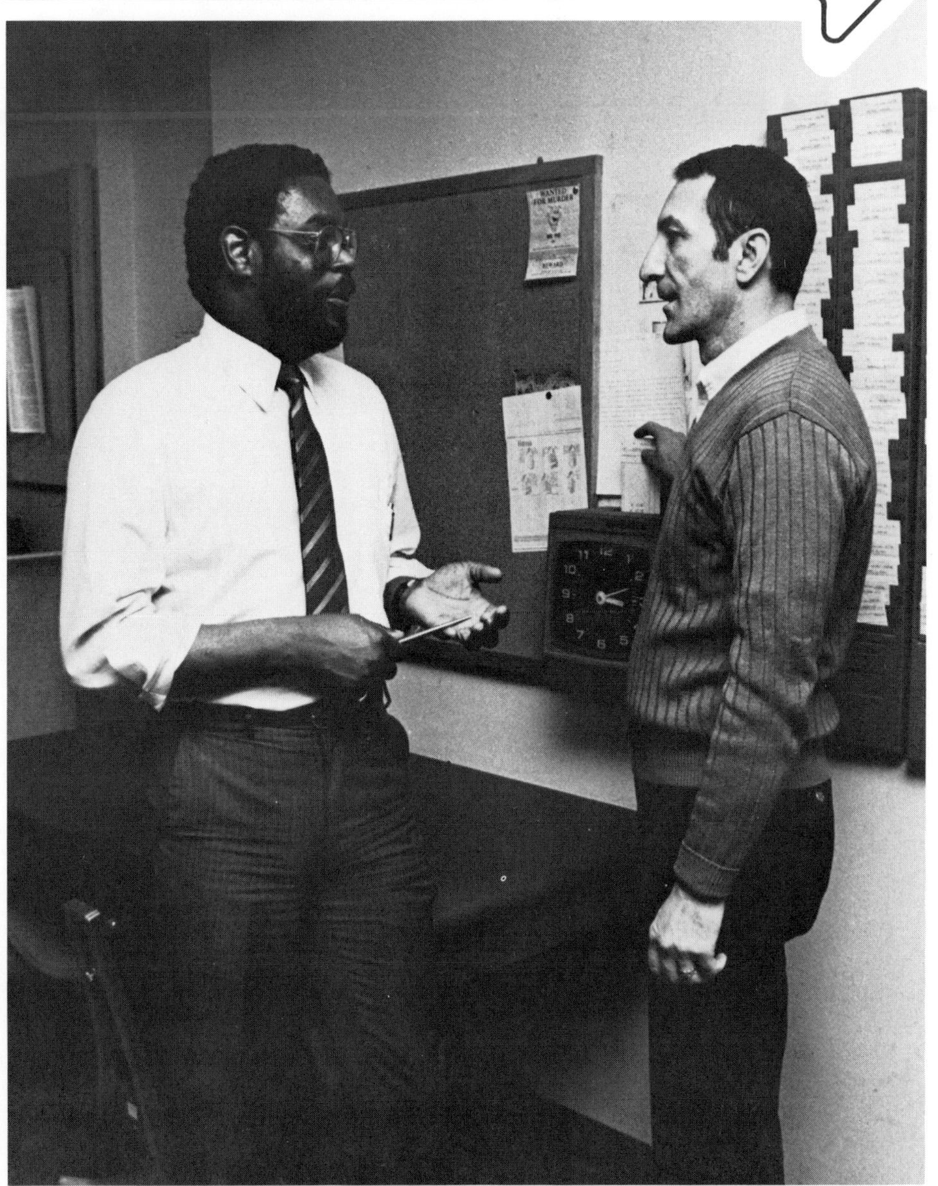

12 • Supporting the Organization

Newly appointed supervisors are sometimes hard put to decide where their loyalties lie. Are they members of management or still part of the work group? The answer is *both*, but the larger part of their support must rest with management. Legally, they are exempt from labor laws and not eligible to strike. This does not mean that they are against their former teammates. What it does mean is that as supervisors they represent both the work group and management to each other and are expected to keep the two operating in harmony.

THE PRIMARY RESPONSIBILITY

The real commitment of supervisors is to the work itself. Their job is to counteract anything that hinders production and to support anything that helps. Management, unions, or workers themselves may take actions that handicap the operation. The supervisor tries to keep things going in spite of insufficient help, low budgets, complicating procedures, unreasonable demands, slowdowns, absenteeism, featherbedding, strikes, and all the other difficulties placed in the way.

Good supervisors do not work against the best interests of their groups. Leaders who take advantage of their position to short-change workers are shortsighted. If the rule on the book states, for example, that supper money is paid when the job runs to six p.m., the supervisor may save a few dollars by stopping the operation 10 minutes earlier, but he or she loses the support and good will of the group. At the same time, supervisors are expected to give their full support to management's aims and objectives. If they have doubts or questions about an action or policy, they state their objections. Once the decision is final, however, they work for its accomplishment.

Cooperation as a Tool

Supervisors are the doers in an organization; they move plans and projects from the paper stage to production. To accomplish this, coordination is required at every step. Effective supervision means most of all the maintenance of good working relations with management, staff, and other supervisors. In some lines of work a close tie with vendors and the public may also be needed. Cooperation is the name of the game.

The first line of cooperation extends to the boss. Supervisors need to keep the next level of management informed at all times. Higher levels should not have to face surprises because they are ignorant of developments. Breakdowns, complaints, problems, jobs behind schedule, suggestions, supply failures, quits, new procedures, policy questions, and any and all changes in the situation should be passed along.

Responses to Management

Supervisors in most cases should have a recommendation for action to be taken. Even when a decision is handed down, they are still expected to raise questions and state problems they see in applying the decision. Managers as a rule do not want "yes men" (or women) working for them. What they want are idea people with reasons for what they advance, but willing to go ahead when the final plan is decided.

Supervisors can move even further in support of the boss. They can back him or her up when challenged and help to make a favorable showing. Chances for them to advance become more readily available if the person above has the way open for moving up.

STAFF DEVELOPMENT

A second duty for supervisors is development of the people under them. They are charged with passing along know-how and leaving a heritage of experience on which younger people can build. Regular coaching and retraining are in order for all members of the group, but special attention should be given to preparing understudies. Promotion is more readily available for those who have their own replacements ready.

Subordinates grow if the leader provides the opportunities. Delegation is the commonly accepted procedure, but there are others. Delegation differs from regular assignments in that the projects worked on are normally part of the supervisor's own job. Maximum freedom is usually given on handling delegated tasks. Progress reports are expected, but methods are left up to the subordinate. Results and procedures can be analyzed later as part of the training. Other techniques for development are talking over problems and decisions with understudies, sending them on observation trips, giving them special assignments, letting them sit in at meetings, and suggesting useful conferences and reading.

One development practice will be carried on whether supervisors know it or not. Their way of handling the job, if successful, will serve as a strong example for subordinates to follow if and when they take over. Good leaders leave something of themselves behind with every organization they serve.

WORKING WITH STAFF

Prima donnas may have their place, but not in business or industry. This is a team operation, not a collection of independent enterprises. When objectives and rules are set for the whole system, supervisors tie their own plans and practices in with the rest. If changes are called for in schedules or budgets or procedures, worthwhile supervisors contribute everything they can. They may raise questions and ask for adjustments to the situation, but they move with the team.

They also maintain sound working relationships with staff. In many organizations experts are available in special fields to advise and assist the line operation. These include computer services, methods people, personnel aides, purchasing and medical staffs, transportation specialists, auditors, engineers, protection services, and many others. All of these can make the work go better, and are there to be used. Only a shortsighted supervisor tries to do everything alone and ignores the help available.

Other Supervisors

Relations with fellow supervisors can be a more complex problem. This will involve all the rivalries of people working competitively in an organization. Stories are familiar of situations in which empire building, back stabbing, and jockeying are common practices.

There can be no hard-and-fast rules on the best conduct to follow in these cases. Needless to say, the strongest and best operated organizations are not characterized by these practices. These organizations proceed on the basis of support among units, open and straightforward exchange at all levels, and a general spirit of cooperation and unity. A supervisor does best to analyze the situation and cut according to the cloth.

A reasonable pattern to follow for those of good will, of course, is straight dealing. With this as a guide, the right move when another supervisor makes a mistake is to try to help rather than carry tales to the boss. The right action when things go wrong in your own case is to take the blame and work with others to straighten it out. Give credit publicly and blame privately. Worry about results and not status. This does not mean becoming a doormat for the organization, but it does mean the kind of dealing on the job that good neighbors practice at home.

PERSONAL DEVELOPMENT

One further responsibility that supervisors bear to the organization is self-development. Supervisors who stand still are really slipping backward while ideas and events move past them. One way they can stay on top of the job is to read trade journals and other publications. Another is to remain open to suggestions from the group and try out their ideas where possible. Courses and conferences can be used as places to pick up ideas and plan improvements. Other supervisors may also have worked out procedures worth copying. A supervisor's failure to adopt these in his or her own situation is often a sign of mistaken pride.

Pointers to Promotion

Many factors can influence an individual's chances of moving up in an organization. It would require a saint and a superman to fill all the qualifications listed as desirable in management literature. The most important condition probably is availability—to be in the right place at the right time. A supervisor's age, training, experience, and capabilities need to be a reasonable fit for the higher-level position when it opens up. The primary abilities required are those of organizing and leading. If these have been proved by past performance, a few additional traits and habits of work will show to advantage when the final selection is made.

Pressure

In addition to availability and a good record, a quality of imperturbability is needed for success in management. Calm behavior under pressure is a requirement for executive placement in this day and age. Upper-level positions bring on stress and tensions that all too often show up in heavy smoking, drinking, insomnia, and compulsive eating. What management wants is individuals with a high boiling point who handle problems and emergencies without panic. When the roof falls in, they are the ones who quietly assess the damage, have the debris cleared up, and direct work to continue in the undamaged sections while they phone in a list of needed services. They are unflappable. When blocked in one direction, they change their approach. Problems are never too big. They break the complex ones down into parts and deal with them one stage at a time. At every turn, they maintain a secure and easy manner with time to talk comfortably as the work moves along.

Commitment

A second key quality sought for promotion is commitment to duty. This has a number of aspects, but the main one is conscientious coverage of the assigned area of service plus concern for the rest of the operation. Supervisors are judged on carrying their share of the load, following through, and reaching out for more. They are considered a good bet if they grab the buck instead of passing it to others.

With these qualifications in good measure, supervisors who fail to move are either up against strong competition or in a spot where openings are scarce. If advancement fails to materialize, they may want to talk over their cases with management. Whatever develops, their attitude toward the organization should continue to be positive. A sour reaction will not improve the situation and may disqualify them for other placement opportunities that develop later.

Support Off the Job

It goes almost without saying that supervisors worth their salt will continue to back their organization in contacts away from the job. They will promote its products or services and avoid negative comments about people or practices back at work. As members of management, their words, if negative, are given extra weight and may cause loss of business or public favor. Transfer of technical information or product developments to competitors is, of course, unethical and in many cases illegal.

Supervisors, along with specialists and other members of management, make up the core of an enterprise. To the extent that they are loyal, progressive, and hard working, and attempt to leave the organization stronger for what they contribute, they serve well in their important capacities. This can mean the difference between just filling a job and being able to show real progress and accomplishment as the measure of a working lifetime.

Check List... supporting the organization

1. Work for the best interests of the group, the manager, and the whole system. Do not put one over the other.

2. First responsibility is to get the work out.

3. Support your own boss. Keep him or her informed. Raise questions but follow through when decisions are final.

4. Build subordinates. Help good people to move ahead. Coach and retrain slow ones.

5. Use staff services. Call in experts as needed.

6. Cooperate with other supervisors. Help on problems. Blame privately; credit publicly.

7. Keep up your field. Strengthen the organization by self-development.

8. Demonstrate sound management qualities in the team effort—commitment to duty and steadiness under pressure.

9. Support the organization off the job. Promote its products or services.

10. Serve in such a way that the operation is stronger for your contribution.

13 · STAYING ON BALANCE

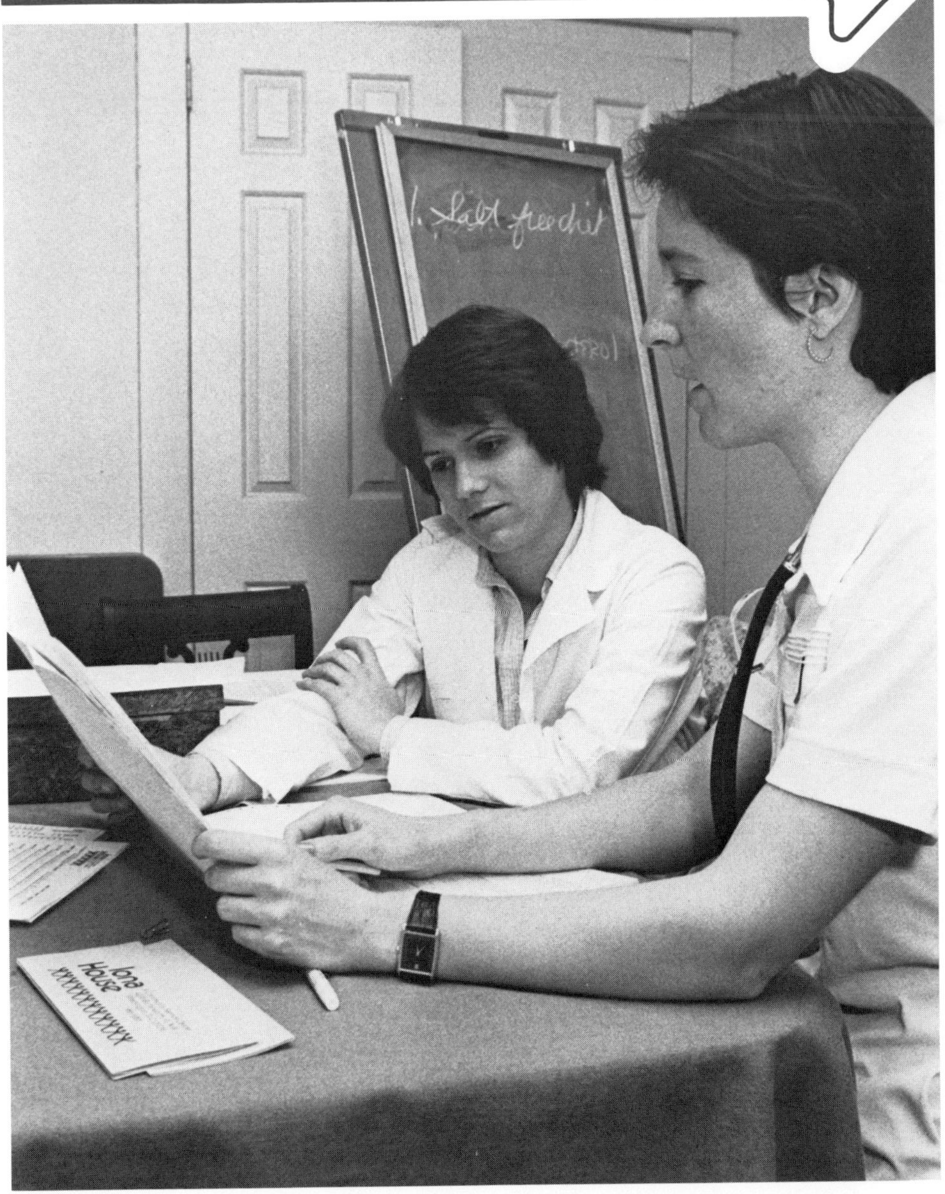

13 • Staying on Balance

Supervisors are promoted out of the ranks mostly because they can organize effectively and work well with others to get the job done. People with these qualities are also needed off the job to handle community projects, club and church activities, and family problems. Everybody wants John (or Jane) Q. Producer to help out, and the demands on time and energy can become a real burden. One of the problems is to carry the load and still keep on balance.

Companies used to look with favor on supervisors who literally lived for the job. They wanted them down at the shop or out in the field nights, weekends, and holidays. This idea has mostly been dropped in modern business operation. Top management still wants major attention given to job problems, but it also recognizes that supervisors are more effective when they have a chance to recharge their batteries. They can then provide stronger leadership and better withstand the pressures of complex work situations.

FOUR DEPARTMENTS OF LIVING

Supervisors are now encouraged to spread their time and energy over four areas of living. One part is still *the job*, with all its requirements for planning and problem solving. The second part is *family and friends*, the ones who are close and make the whole effort worthwhile. The third is *community service*, the larger needs of society outside the private circle. The fourth is the *personal area*, which takes in rest, recreation, and self-development. Supervisors who divide their activities along these lines acquire a strength and balance that enables them to ride through problems at work with steady assurance.

Health Habits

Contrary to some workers' opinions, supervisors are human. They are troubled by the same physical and mental upsets as others, but they carry more of a responsibility for keeping these under control. By regular attendance and an energetic approach to the work they set an example for the groups they lead.

Maintenance of health and fitness is part of the supervisor's personal area of living, but it affects all the others. The key to success here is also found in a moderate and balanced approach. Reasonable rest, recreation, and attention to medical counsel are parts of the recipe.

Personal Growth

People learn rapidly when young and reach out for new ideas and experiences. Then comes the time, unless they watch themselves, when they stop learning and level off on a plateau of self-satisfaction. They cease growing and go to seed.

These are not the makings of an effective supervisor. What is wanted is a man or woman who keeps moving, not at the same pace as earlier but still actively. Employees like to serve under an alert and progressive leader, and management looks for the same qualities in determining likely candidates for advancement. Success in supervision comes most often for the individual who stays open to suggestions and is willing to move in new directions. Balance, however, is important in this also. Changes should be made only after study and testing, not blindly and on impulse.

Community Service

In reviewing the four departments of living most people can understand the need for and satisfaction of spending time with family and friends. But why take on extra outside responsibilities? The reason is that times have changed. Most business organizations today are community-minded. They recognize the benefits of having their people involved in civic and volunteer work. Supervisors who are active in their communities put plus marks on their records with the company. In addition, they get useful experience in planning projects, influencing groups, directing programs, speaking in public, and otherwise developing personal competence. And they have the satisfaction of serving worthwhile causes and contributing to the betterment of the community.

Satisfying as all these activities may be, they still need to be balanced against other demands. Too many problems on and off the job can begin to take their toll. People have different tolerances and need to gauge what they can handle comfortably. Time is the big problem here.

HANDLING TIME PRESSURES

"Fail to manage time and time will manage you!" This is a common business expression and states the cause for many a failure. When supervisors begin to rush around aimlessly or try to cover the whole job themselves, the operation soon starts downhill. Such leaders give as much attention to details as they do to major problems. Instead of serving as captain of the ship, they pull up the anchor, start the engine, chart the course, stand watch, and run the galley on the side. Meanwhile the crew play cards, swap stories, read comic books, and keep out of the way. This is no pattern for running a ship or job operation of any kind.

Differences in Time Use

There are several kinds of work time, and the differences are important. One is *employee time*, used for following routines and doing assigned jobs. A second is system time, which involves all the record keeping, reports, meetings, and contacts that go into organizational living. A third is *supervising time*, spent on overseeing the work, training, problem solving, and communicating. And last is *improvement time*, which is where the real points are made. This is time spent analyzing work flow, planning ahead, and developing improved methods and procedures.

Supervisors do best when they avoid employee work and minimize system demands. The main thrust of their effort is best directed toward supervision and work improvement. In other words, they spend their time where it counts. The price they pay otherwise is strain and fatigue leading to weak coverage of the job and eventual breakdown.

Balance

All of these points on health, home, time, and community service are mentioned here because they can make trouble for the supervisor. The complex conditions under which operations are carried out today call for men and women who can concentrate their best abilities on the problems they face. To the extent they can stay in control and on balance, they are ready to supervise.

Check List . . .
staying on balance

1. Recognize that demands on you can become heavy.

2. Carry the load and still stay on balance.

3. Spread time and energy over four areas: job, home, community, and self.

4. Put health habits first. Recipe is rest, recreation, and medical care.

5. Maintain mental alertness—try new ideas and experiences, continue to grow.

6. Serve the community. Balance this against other demands.

7. Make wise use of time. Concentrate on *supervising* and *improving* the work situation.

8. Take an even, steady approach to the job and outside pressures.

14· THIS IS SUPERVISION

14 • This Is Supervision

The most demanding and frustrating job in the whole list of occupations.

And the most rewarding, challenging, and satisfying.

A position of trust and responsibility with influence over the security, income, opportunity, and peace of mind of every member of the group.

A leadership function charged with building and shaping a collection of employees into a producing unit with pride and satisfaction in their work.

A pressure post between orders and instructions from management, problems and complaints from workers, delays and excuses from suppliers, reports and reminders from staff, and demands and directives from government and the unions.

And still an operation that gets the work out on time and on standard.

A job that calls for all the skills and knowledge of a psychologist, engineer, actor, chaplain, mathematician, physician, communicator, manager, coach, and mechanic.

Plus the wisdom of Solomon and the patience of Job.

There is no finer calling and no service greater in importance than the direction of a productive work team contributing to the economic needs and general welfare of the nation.

If you are ready for the assignment . . . **START SUPERVISING!**

658302
S559

SHOUT HOWARD

START SUPERVI

COPY 1

VOLUME

PART

EDITION 3

YEAR 1984

CONTROL NO. 872214

COST 14.79